1-TO 1
LEARNING

Laptop Programs
That Work

WITHDRAWN

Pamela Livingston

International Society for Technology in Education
EUGENE, OREGON • WASHINGTON, DC

1-TO-1 LEARNING
Laptop Programs That Work

Pamela Livingston

Director of Publishing
Jean Marie Hall

Acquisitions and Development Editor
Scott Harter

Production Editor
Lynda Gansel

Rights and Permissions Administrator
Diane Durrett

Production Coordinator
Maddelyn High

Copy Editor
Nancy Olson

Book and Cover Design
Kim McGovern

Layout and Production
Kim McGovern

International Society for Technology in Education (ISTE)
Washington, DC, Office:
1710 Rhode Island Ave., NW, Suite 900, Washington, DC 20036

Eugene, Oregon, Office:
175 West Broadway, Suite 300, Eugene, OR 97401-3003
Order Desk: 1.800.336.5191
Order Fax: 1.541.302.3778
Customer Service: orders@iste.org
Book Publishing: books@iste.org
Rights and Permissions: permissions@iste.org
Web site: www.iste.org

First Edition
ISBN 10: 1-56484-225-8
ISBN 13: 978-1-56484-225-1

ABOUT ISTE

The International Society for Technology in Education (ISTE) is a nonprofit professional organization with a worldwide membership of leaders in education technology. We are dedicated to promoting appropriate uses of technology to support and improve learning, teaching, and administration in PK–12 and teacher education. As part of that mission, ISTE provides high-quality and timely information, services, and materials, such as this book.

ISTE Book Publishing works with experienced educators to develop and produce practical resources for classroom teachers, teacher educators, and technology leaders. Every manuscript we select for publication is carefully peer-reviewed and professionally edited. We look for content that emphasizes the effective use of technology where it can make a difference—increasing the productivity of teachers and administrators; helping students with unique learning styles, abilities, or backgrounds; collecting and using data for decision making at the school and district levels; and creating dynamic, project-based learning environments that engage 21st-century learners. We value your feedback on this book and other ISTE products. E-mail us at **books@iste.org**.

ISTE is home of the National Educational Technology Standards (NETS) Project, the National Educational Computing Conference (NECC), and the National Center for Preparing Tomorrow's Teachers to Use Technology (NCPT[3]). To find out more about these and other ISTE initiatives and to view our complete book list or request a print catalog, visit our Web site at **www.iste.org**. You'll find information about:

▶ ISTE, our mission, and our members

▶ Membership opportunities and services

▶ Online communities and special interest groups (SIGS)

▶ Professional development services

▶ Research and evaluation services

▶ Educator resources

▶ ISTE's National Educational Technology Standards (NETS) for Students, Teachers, and Administrators

▶ *Learning & Leading with Technology* magazine

▶ *Journal of Research on Technology in Education*

ABOUT THE AUTHOR

Pamela Livingston has held computer support positions at Pan American World Airways and Chemical Bank and served as a project leader at PC Magazine Labs and a technical editor for *PC Sources Magazine*. More than a dozen years ago, she turned to educational computer support, and in 2002 became head of technology at The Peck School in Morristown, New Jersey. At Peck, she teaches middle school students, steers the technology program (including Peck's 1-to-1 laptop initiative), and manages the IT department. Livingston was a member of edACCESS's steering committee, served on DEVTec's executive committee, and is a member of the NAIS technology task force. She has presented at many education technology conferences, including NECC, Irving (Texas) ISD's One-to-One Symposium, and the Lausanne Collegiate Laptop Institute. Her published articles have appeared in *PC Magazine, PC Sources Magazine, Learning and Leading with Technology, The New York Law Journal*, and *Computer Buyer's Guide*. She holds a BS in computer systems from the City University of New York and an MS in education and technology from Chestnut Hill College in Philadelphia.

Acknowledgments

I want to thank the many educators nationwide who have given generously of their time and have provided me with such wonderful insights into the possibilities and challenges of 1-to-1 implementation. We all benefit from hearing stories about how things work for others: why certain approaches were chosen, how students and teachers were affected, and what was learned in hindsight. The stories these practitioners graciously shared with me represent the real meat of this book. Without the dedication, professionalism, and hard work of the educators who have pioneered laptop programs in their schools and districts, this book would not have been possible. I hope the passion of these education technology leaders has been adequately conveyed in these pages.

I also want to thank the teachers and administrators at The Peck School for all the help they've given me. I'd especially like to thank Elisabeth Fraser, whose vision for the seamless integration of technology into the curriculum served as the impetus for Peck's laptop program. Her steady leadership guided the laptop program from its inception to the healthy, vital state it's in now. The support of Peck School's technology department, administration, board of trustees, faculty, staff, and students has been critical to the success of this project. The school takes its mission of being a "family school" into the classroom and halls every day, and I feel very fortunate to be a part of that family.

Finally, I want to thank the International Society for Technology in Education for its support of this book, and Scott Harter, my editor, for seeing the potential of 1-to-1 computing and helping to guide this book to its completion.

Dedication

1-to-1 Learning is dedicated to my daughter, Annie, a terrific writer.

CONTENTS

PREFACE

My Story

In May 2004, I graduated from Chestnut Hill College in Philadelphia with an MS in education and technology. My thesis project was a qualitative case study of the technology use and skills of seventh-grade students at The Peck School in Morristown, New Jersey, where I am head of technology. Truly a labor of love, this project allowed me to interview bright, articulate students to find out how they studied and learned with computers.

Seventh- and eighth-grade students at The Peck School have enjoyed 1-to-1 access to laptop computers since 1998. As I pursued my thesis research, I began to wonder what influence this ubiquitous access was having on students' studying and learning. I also wondered how having a powerful "digital assistant" of their very own might be affecting their learning. Might 1-to-1 access be enhancing the development of metacognitive thinking skills? By the end of my research, I was convinced that this was, indeed, the case for the small sample of students I interviewed.

As educators, we create and assess academic work and provide students with tools to do that work. My research brought home to me the paramount importance of those tools and the impact they can have on student performance. Why shouldn't we give students the best and most effective tools to do the work we want them to accomplish? Even more important, if we give students advanced tools and observe how they use them to organize and challenge themselves, what will this tell us about teaching and learning that we haven't even envisioned?

These are the insights and questions that led me to write *1-to-1 Learning: Laptop Programs That Work*. My experience writing this book and interviewing scores of people who have planned and implemented 1-to-1 programs across the country has only reinforced my convictions about the cognitive and educational value of ubiquitous access to technology. Putting a computer in the hands of every child—24 hours a day, 7 days a week—is key to meaningful, effective integration of technology in education.

Introduction

SCHOOL LAPTOP PROGRAMS MAKE A DIFFERENCE IN LEARNING

AFTER A YEAR SPENT REVIEWING COUNTLESS STUDIES and interviewing scores of education technologists from the United States, Canada, Europe, and Australia, I find myself returning to the same question all educators tend to ask when confronted with a new education technology or practice: Why?

Why write a book about laptop programs in K–12 schools? The answer comes back clear as a bell: because school laptop programs can make a difference in learning. It's because we, as educators, parents, and adult learners, can partner with children through technology to help them become better thinkers and problem solvers. If the front-end device used for information gathering and analysis can help streamline information processing, then it stands to reason that the vital back-end problem-solving and critical thinking can happen quicker and easier.

Nearly every study I read showed that laptops can increase student motivation and engagement, and when motivation to learn increases, so does the retention of that learning. When we see our students immersed in a sea of technology—as they so clearly are in our 21st-century world—it's our duty as educators to help them navigate it smoothly, effectively, and purposefully. It's a responsibility we cannot avoid, and a job that's made much easier when all students have their own "digital assistant."

What Is a Digital Assistant?

Throughout this book, I use the term "digital assistant" (or sometimes "learning assistant") to refer to laptop and handheld computers used for learning. My reasons for doing so can be found in an article titled "Student Laptop Computers in Classrooms—Not Just a Tool" (Nair, 2000). In it, Prakash Nair states:

> I have started referring to computers in classrooms as "digital teaching assistants"... [my use of this term] is derived from what experts say and from my own personal observation of the way children interact with computers. It is also an accurate description of what computers do for children within and outside the classroom.

Nair goes on to describe how a tool can help with the completion of an activity but how an "assistant" can support thinking and learning in a much broader way than a tool can. A tool has a single, primary purpose. For example, a hammer is expressly designed for pounding nails. Computers, on the other hand, can serve myriad purposes: writing, reading, studying, learning, researching, organizing, making assumptions, solving problems, publishing, presenting, connecting ideas, and creating new ways of understanding. Thus, the importance and usefulness of laptop computers for learning goes far beyond the single purpose implied by those who would call them "just a tool."

A digital assistant can serve as a database for work and files, a sketchpad and planner for projects, a publisher for reports and papers, and a conduit for research that provides access to online resources. It's a communication facilitator for e-mail, instant messaging, and blogging; a calculator and what-if analyzer of data and information; and a digital processor for photos and video. It's a device that facilitates a student's thinking, analyzing, presenting, writing, reading, researching, revising, communicating, questioning, proposing, creating, surmising, and publishing.

A digital assistant offers much more functionality than any single tool, even a Swiss Army Knife. Students armed with digital assistants have an advantage over those students without them. They can expand on their studies, demonstrate and communicate their understanding and learning, retrieve and process data and information, communicate more precisely, and create presentations and products with greater substance and style.

Who Needs a Digital Assistant?

The world as a whole increasingly requires flexible, adaptable synthesizers of information who are discerning users of technology tools. Those who are fluent in the kinds of interconnected, collaborative work processes that these tools support and encourage have a distinct advantage in today's job market. There's a reason that terms such as "information technology" have gradually replaced the old term "data processing": data is just raw numbers and facts, but information is what is needed to solve problems, connect ideas, make decisions, and create new products and services. Information is data that has been made useful and usable for whatever comes next.

We need to provide our children with the ability to transform raw data and facts into information that can be put to use. The current generation of students—the so-called "millennials" born from 1982 to 2000—are already swimming daily in a sea of ubiquitous media and technology. So it only makes sense that we seek to use those same technologies to support that process.

Mike Muir, one of the architects of Maine's successful statewide laptop program, is among many experts who believe that students today are innately multitaskers. According to this view, the current generation of students finds it very natural to learn in an environment where they're constantly surrounded by multiple inputs and sources of information. Most teachers, on the other hand, are "unitaskers." They view this kind of multimedia environment as being distracting and not conducive to learning. This difference, Dr. Muir says (personal communication, October 2, 2005), holds both sides back:

Many of us (teachers) are unitaskers—we need to focus on one thing at a time and feel frustrated and anxious when we're being forced to do too many things at once. When we see our students working on more than one thing at a time, we worry that they aren't paying attention, or that they'll shut down because they have too much going on at one time. But many of our students are multitaskers, who comfortably work on multiple things at the same time. The mistake we sometimes make, however, is thinking that we are helping them by having them focus on only one thing at a time, when in reality a multitasker can feel as frustrated and anxious when asked to focus on only one thing as a unitasker does when asked to perform multiple things at once.

Are we as adults trying to adapt today's children to a unitasking mode of learning that is unnatural for them to emulate? Outside of school, millennials are constantly using cell phones, texting their friends, listening to music, playing multiuser games online—in other words, accessing a broad range of media and information all at the same time. Can we hold them back and make them more like us? *Should* we hold them back and insist that they learn the way we've learned when multitasking clearly works well for them?

Some say today's multitasking millennials can share computers and still enjoy all the benefits computers have to offer. Banks of four or five computers have been installed in many classrooms around the country, and most schools have computer labs. So don't we already have enough computers for writing papers and getting projects done?

Here's the rub with that argument: because we've long known that students need to work at their own pace and in their own way, both at school and at home, no one expects students to stand in line or adhere to a schedule for using technologies such as books, pencils, or calculators. However, that's precisely what we're asking them to do when it comes to computers, the most powerful education technology of all. We provide (or require parents to provide) books and paper and writing utensils and expect each student to bring these tools to class and be ready to work. Since computers can do so much more than these tools to support learning, why have we been so slow to make them available to every student in every classroom? Yes, computers are costly, but is cost really the most important issue here? Or is our reluctance to embrace computers in the classroom a function of our generational inability to understand the needs and learning habits of the millennials?

If students are given access to computers only once or twice a week, in a separate room and without all the resources of the classroom, technology integration is simply not possible. If computers are something extra that's used occasionally for curricular enhancement and as a reward for good behavior, technology integration is not possible. Technology integration—not technology for technology's sake, but technology integration—isn't possible unless it's woven appropriately into everything a student or teacher does in the classroom. True technology integration requires 1-to-1 access—the same level of access to technology that most students take for granted outside of school and that our plugged-in world increasingly requires of all of its citizens.

Ubiquitous Computing

Many experts believe that ubiquitous computing is the answer to our current generation of information-craving students. The term "ubiquitous computing" was coined in the early 1990s by the late Mark Weiser (1993), who defined it as follows:

> Ubiquitous computing is the method of enhancing computer use by making many computers available throughout the physical environment, but making them effectively invisible to the user.

Weiser's initial vision involved the use of "tabs" that could be programmed to access information and help with school and home life, but this isn't exactly what has happened. We aren't waking up to view "electronic trails" from our neighbor's comings and goings (as Weiser described), nor do we look around our office for the visual tab displaying "fresh coffee." Weiser imagined multiple computing devices all around our environment that would be transparent and unobtrusive. He envisioned several stages, or "tiers," of this future, calling the final one "calm computing." Shortly before his death in 1999, he indicated that we were just beginning to move toward this final tier.

While we aren't there yet, most of us would agree that computers are a ubiquitous presence in our everyday lives. Students who learn how to use computers effectively when they're young are more successful when it comes to higher education or securing a job. Even now, it's difficult to find a position in the workforce that doesn't require some form of computer use.

Elisabeth Fraser, my predecessor as head of technology at The Peck School, relates (personal communication, August 6, 2005) that the graduate students she now hires are never more than 5 feet away from their computers, which they use for communication, thinking, analyzing, writing, and researching. This kind of ubiquitous use, and the comfort level and confidence in technology that it requires, doesn't just happen overnight. If we encourage our children to develop these skills early in their academic lives, think how much better prepared they'll be for every leg of their educational and occupational journey.

The advantages of giving students a laptop computer for home and school use—24 hours a day, 7 days a week—are many. It means no more waiting in line for access, no more lab scheduling bottlenecks, no more need to move to another room or building to do a research project or Internet search. Dr. Muir described to me (personal communication, August 4, 2005) how one group of Maine students used their laptops to learn about Christopher Columbus' voyages to America. One student who wondered how big the ships were went online to find out, then showed the results to all the other students. They then went out to the hallway and mapped out the approximate size of the three ships. They were amazed at how small these three ships that carried over 90 people across the ocean really were, and gained new insights into the communicable diseases suffered by the passengers during the voyage. This student-led teachable moment would not have been possible if the student had not had his own computer readily available in the classroom.

Most of the laptop programs described in this book allow students to take the computers home with them, though some schools and districts provide laptops only during the school day. In my opinion, however, the magic numbers are 1-to-1 and 24/7. When the laptop becomes a constant companion and a primary resource for information and communication, students become vested in caring for it and learning how to use it more effectively.

While not all the details of Weiser's vision have come to pass, few would argue that we have, indeed, entered into a ubiquitous computing age. Today, we can use the Internet to find information on nearly everything—and almost instantly. We can collaborate with colleagues in real time or asynchronously, view shared information on SmartBoards, and use wikis and blogs to communicate and co-create with people we haven't even met. Our cars and traffic lights can speak to us, all our banking can be done online, and we can access maps, books, and online shopping malls from coffee shops, airports, and hotel rooms. Ubiquitous computing is already here, and it's critical that we, as educators, respond to the changes it has made—and will continue to make—in the lives of our students.

Getting to the Thinking Faster

Educators want students to synthesize information, not just repeat it back. We want them to think, not just memorize facts and demonstrate skills. Since the typical school day is divided into fairly short segments of time, ranging from 35 minutes to 1 hour, helping kids absorb facts more efficiently and encouraging more higher order thinking in the classroom is a challenge teachers in all content areas face. 1-to-1 access to computers can definitely help.

If it takes 40 minutes for an environmental science class to gather weather data from atlases and almanacs and turn it into pencil and paper charts, how much time is left to think about what the chart is saying? How much time is there to consider "what if" scenarios, such as, "What if the mean temperature rose by 10 degrees?" Equipped with a laptop computer, access to the Internet, and a spreadsheet/graphing program, however, students can quickly find and analyze current data. They can plug that data into spreadsheet templates, and prepare charts for half a dozen different "what if" scenarios in the same amount of time it would take to make a pencil and paper chart. Personal digital assistants allow students to get to the thinking faster.

This is an important idea because it helps answer critics who ask, "Why spend money on computers for students?" Supplying every student with a digital assistant provides a real, tangible benefit. Almost everyone will agree that a word-processed paper trumps a handwritten one, if only because it makes revisions so much easier. Think of the bad ol' days when students had to handwrite or type every paper for every course. Every time they wanted to make a change or correct an error, they had to start all over again if they wanted to present a clean copy to the teacher. Multiply that by every writing assignment or project a student worked on over the course of 12 years, and the result was hours and hours of tedious copying, most of it resulting in no appreciable new insights or learning.

With a computer, a student has immediate access to search engines, spreadsheets, online databases, and myriad other resources. They can help them gather and analyze information; synthesize, draft, and revise the response to it; and present the results in a clean, professional document that is much easier for teachers to read and evaluate. Computers help students become infinitely more productive, providing extra time for them to develop the higher order thinking skills that we all agree are crucial to success in higher education and beyond. Computers empower students to get to the thinking faster.

Are Laptops About to "Tip"?

In his book *The Tipping Point: How Little Things Can Make a Big Difference*, Gladwell (2000) describes how a trend or an idea starts out small and then "tips," becoming ubiquitous. Are we nearing the tipping point for laptop programs in schools? It's possible, given how many public and private schools have invested the time, money, and resources into building 1-to-1 programs for their students.

In the most recent report from the National Center for Educational Statistics (Parsad & Jones, 2005), 8% of surveyed schools indicated they had some type of laptop program already in place, and another 6% were planning programs. By now, then, there should be more than 14,000 public schools (and thousands of independent and parochial schools) nationwide with laptop programs. If we compare these numbers to the growth in school Internet access over the past 9 years (from 35% of schools to nearly 100%), it would seem that conditions are right for 1-to-1 programs to tip sometime in the next 5 to 7 years.

One current initiative that may cause this tipping to happen much faster is MIT's $100 laptop initiative, led by Dr. Nicholas Negroponte, Dr. Seymour Papert (see interview, next page), and Dr. Joseph Jacobson. These researchers and five corporate sponsors have formed a nonprofit organization, called One Laptop Per Child (OLPC), which plans to introduce a prototype of a $100, wireless, Internet-ready laptop in early 2007.

Preliminary drawings show an extremely durable laptop equipped with both an AC adapter and either a hand crank or a foot pump, for powering the laptop when no electrical outlets are available. The hand crank will provide 10 minutes of power for every 1 minute of cranking—an extremely useful accommodation for rural students in poorer countries around the world, where the first models will be shipped. While the OLPC initiative will focus initially on meeting the needs of developing nations, it will likely spur similar initiatives and products in the United States and Europe. Massachusetts has already requested 500,000 of the OLPC laptops, and other states have expressed interest as well.

Assuming that OLPC will be able to follow through on the number of laptops they've promised each country, this $100 laptop program will have long-range implications for the development of information technology skills around the world. The question then becomes how the United States will react to the global competition that will surely ensue.

Who Should Read This Book?

1-to-1 Learning has been written for administrators, teachers, parents, researchers, and anyone whose school or school district is considering a laptop program. It can also serve the needs of educators who work in schools or districts that already have a laptop program but want to see what other schools have done and are doing. This book provides teachers with dozens of real-world stories describing how laptops have been used to transform teaching and learning. Parents can discover how students use laptops to deepen their learning and expand their horizons. Administrators will find the sections on planning, professional development, and logistics particularly useful as they steward their own laptop programs. Anyone considering a laptop program will find a host of anecdotes, ideas, lessons learned, and challenges overcome, each of which will be helpful as decisions are made.

INTERVIEW WITH DR. SEYMOUR PAPERT ON THE OLPC INITIATIVE

Q: How has Maine's 1-to-1 laptop program informed your thinking about one laptop per child, and how will that experience shape your influence on the $100 laptop program?

A: I got a unique general education in large-scale 1-to-1 from participating in all stages of the Maine program: initial conception, fierce political battles, implementation, disappointments. Numerous little lessons acquired from this will be useful, but I can mention a specific big one from each of the four stages: 1) Start with visionary political leaders rather than with educators. 2) Expect opposition and know that it can be beaten. 3) Expect the toughest educational challenges to come not from opponents but from supporters of the idea, who tame and dilute its impact in order to make it work smoothly. 4) Present from the outset the adoption of one per child as a multiyear ramp-up process.

I also learned that it's an illusion to make the transition easier by interpreting "per child" as "per seventh- or eighth-grader." For OLPC, child means child.

Q: Massachusetts is reportedly requesting 500,000 of the units. Are other states also interested, and if so, will the OLPC initiative grow to accommodate this?

A: OLPC's current model is based on partnerships with governments. Strategies for states, districts, individual schools, and so on are still developing but could take several shapes. Perhaps OLPC will expand the definition of government to include other entities; more likely it will cooperate with companies to make a commercial version. Another possibility is that the OLPC example will incite the independent development of different low-cost machines. If this happens, we'll say, "More power to them," rather than see them as competition. The goal of OLPC is not to dominate the market for hardware or software but to see computers get into the hands of the children of the world.

Q: What educational material will come with the laptops?

A: The OLPC is not trying to reinvent the curriculum for its partner countries. The machines will come with general-purpose tools designed to make it easy for each of them to find its own path to new forms of education. We will, however, exert a constructionist influence by providing a child-accessible programming system in the spirit of Logo and Squeak. We're also working hard to make the operating system and basic suite of applications far more intelligible and self-explanatory than, say, those of the currently used systems. We expect that as a result, the level of understanding, by students and teachers, of the computers and of computational thinking will be substantially higher than in any of the large-scale 1-to-1 projects in the so-called developed countries.

Several research studies on the design and implementation of 1-to-1 laptop programs have been incorporated into the guidelines presented in this book. You'll find studies by Rockman *et al*, Maine's Learning Technology Initiative, the Laptops for Learning Task Force, the Laptop Initiative at Athens Academy in Georgia, Beaufort County (South Carolina) School District, EDC's Center for Children and Technology, Henrico County

(Virginia) School District, and Michigan's Freedom to Learn. These studies are referenced in appendix B. You can also find links to nearly every study by going to the Ubiquitous Computing Evaluation Consortium Web site at www.ubiqcomputing.org. It's a great, well-organized starting point that contains research, templates, and wisdom from laptop pioneers.

As with any new education initiative, many people work on the front lines, charged with coordinating the day-to-day effort that goes into providing ubiquitous access to students. I've conducted interviews with several dozen leaders whose generous and honest responses form the basis for most of the stories and examples in this book. The many different ways educators have planned and carried out laptop programs in schools both large and small is inspiring, and rich with insights into the possibilities of 1-to-1.

The book has three parts, and can be sampled or read from start to finish.

Part 1 describes what a 1-to-1 laptop program can mean for students, teachers, and schools. It begins with an overview of the laptop program at The Peck School. It then looks at similar programs at The Denver School of Science and Technology, The Urban School in San Francisco, and Whitfield School in St. Louis, Missouri. Next, it surveys three large-scale laptop programs—Maine's, Michigan's, and Henrico County School District's—and ends with a review of research on the effects of 1-to-1 access on teaching and learning in K–12 schools.

Part 2 delves into the nuts and bolts of planning and implementing a laptop program and the individual components that can make them or break them.

Part 3 looks at how laptops can change the teaching and learning environment and how teachers and administrators can effectively manage the 1-to-1 classroom and make the most of ubiquitous access

A number of useful resources are gathered in the appendices. These include a model acceptable use policy (AUP); a laptop-specific AUP; an assessment sheet for laptops; a list of professional resources for laptop programs; a glossary of terms and acronyms; and ISTE's National Educational Technology Standards (NETS).

A Final Word Before We Begin

A laptop program is an expensive, complex undertaking, with no real end in sight once you commit to the journey. Most of us who have started down this road believe that the considerable time and energy we've put into our programs have been well worth it.

This doesn't necessarily mean that a laptop program is right for every school and every district. Only those with a firm grasp of a school's or district's mission, culture, and direction can determine if providing 1-to-1 access is the right thing for their students and teachers.

One thing you can count on, however: change will happen if you provide every student and teacher with a laptop. Learning from the mistakes and successes of educators who have gone before you is the surest way to guarantee that those changes will be for the better.

Part One

1-TO-1 PROGRAMS THAT WORK

AMAZING AND POWERFUL THINGS happen when students have a digital assistant at their fingertips to help them learn. Giving every student a laptop computer opens up an entirely new set of opportunities for both collaborative and self-directed learning. The educational paradigm shift that proponents of technology have long promised can become a reality when students have 1-to-1 access. The chapters in part 1 reveal the possibilities of that paradigm shift by looking at successful 1-to-1 programs from around the country.

We're a species of storytellers and story listeners, and some of our best learning comes from hearing what others have experienced, especially the challenges they've faced and the lessons they've learned. So the stories that follow can teach us much about the possibilities of 1-to-1 laptops. Each story reflects the unique factors—pedagogy, mission, demographics, teaching philosophies, and funding—that determined the particular implementation strategies these pioneering programs adopted. We're fortunate to be able to learn from so many thoughtful educators who have started down the 1-to-1 road before us.

One of the most important things I've learned as I worked on this book is how the same basic hardware—laptop computers—can serve equally well the needs of schools and districts with very different goals and demographics. For instance, the Forney (Texas) Independent School District is one of the fastest growing districts in the country and faces a huge challenge each year when it comes to ordering textbooks. Books must be ordered in the spring for the following fall, but when September rolls around, the number of children attending a particular school may have doubled. How then to provide enough textbooks for all the students without having them wait months for reordered books to arrive?

Forney's answer has been to provide their fifth- and sixth-graders with e-textbooks that can be accessed with school-issued laptops. Once the school district has obtained the e-book license, it's a simple matter to update the license count and burn as many CDs as needed. Forney is even pushing the envelope a little bit and negotiating directly with publishers who don't yet offer e-books. Plus, by encouraging laptop use in the classroom, Forney has set the stage for teachers to try new approaches and integrate technology more effectively into their curriculum.

Maine was motivated to institute a first-of-its-kind statewide laptop program for a whole different set of reasons. Angus King, former governor of Maine, wanted to produce a more technologically literate populace to help the state compete for new jobs in the information age (Peterson, 2000). Once educators took over the project that he started, these two goals morphed into specific teaching and learning goals. Both sets of goals have been reached with the help of 1-to-1 access. Maine is now producing more tech-savvy graduates, and the classroom experience in Maine has undergone a sea change.

Meanwhile, St. Thomas Episcopal School in Tampa, Florida, had the goal of implementing more differentiated learning for their students. They believed they could serve their students better if they grouped them according to learning styles and pace. Teachers were given considerable professional development and instruction on the philosophy and implementation of differentiated learning. They also were given laptops. Soon they began creating projects that allowed students to work on different aspects of a single, overarching activity, grouped according to the individual students' abilities and development levels.

1-to-1 laptops made this move to differentiated learning possible. In a traditional setting, resources are spread thin when several groups are working on the same project. If, for instance, the library has 10 copies of a particular book, it is almost inevitable that 11 or more students will need that same book. Add to that the different abilities and development levels of students, and a teacher's ability to provide every student with the resources needed to research, analyze, and present on a given topic is often quite limited.

When each student in each group is equipped with a laptop, on the other hand, student-directed projects can be taken to a new level. The need to share limited resources is no longer an issue, and every student can present and publish at a developmentally appropriate level. Students get to the thinking faster when they have their own digital assistants to help them.

Previewing the Chapters

The first chapter tells the story of The Peck School. A traditional, independent school that's been in operation for more than 100 years, Peck has administered for the past 8 years a 1-to-1 laptop program for its seventh- and eighth-grade students. The Peck School embarked early on this trend toward ubiquitous access, forming stakeholder partnerships and learning lessons along the way.

Chapter 2 looks at several school and classroom laptop programs. The first school surveyed is The Urban School in San Francisco. Student-centered and progressive, Urban has achieved great success and curricular vitality through laptops. Whitfield School in St. Louis and its unique process-oriented approach to technology is profiled next. The Denver School of Science and Technology, which has provided laptops for all of its teachers and students from the moment it opened its doors, is the final school profiled.

Chapter 3 describes some larger-scale laptop programs, such as those currently running in Maine, Michigan, and Henrico County (Virginia) Public Schools. These stories offer rich insights into the challenges of implementing a district-wide or statewide 1-to-1 program.

Chapter 4 presents current research on the effectiveness of 1-to-1 programs and summarizes what these studies reveal about teaching and learning with ubiquitous technology. Studies from Maine, the Beaufort County School District in South Carolina, and the Athens Academy in Athens, Georgia (among others) provide both quantitative and qualitative data on how laptops can change schools.

A Framework for 1-to-1 Success: EPC

As I reviewed the principles and strategies employed by the many different laptop programs profiled in this book, it became clear to me that three traits above all others seemed to separate the successful programs from those that encountered more challenges. I've tried to capture those traits in a conceptual framework that goes by the acronym **EPC**.

The **E** in EPC is for **Educators**. For a laptop program to be successful, **Educators** must be at the helm, whether they be education professors, K–12 teachers, or school administrators. Educators need to be on the front lines in the classroom, of course, but they should also take the lead in the strategy and implementation meetings in which a laptop program is planned, steered, assessed, and renewed year after year. Without the **E**, the program won't get off the ground properly, and the tremendous potential of 1-to-1 won't be effectively realized.

The **P** is for **Planning**, which is often the area given shortest shrift. Considerable planning needs to happen before a single laptop is purchased. Jumping on the laptop bandwagon without a clear idea of where that wagon is heading will result in frustration at the very least, and total chaos and failure if you're really unlucky.

C represents **Commitment**. Educators need to be committed to the success of the overall program and do their part to make it happen. This commitment means believing in the results even though challenges will arise and time-honored habits and traditions will change. To be successful, all stakeholders must be equally committed to providing their piece of the laptop puzzle: hardware, software, network infrastructure, logistics, professional development, and classroom implementation.

Schools and districts moving ahead with a laptop initiative should consider how they're structuring their program to facilitate each of these crucial elements. If, for instance, your school's technology plan is full of technical acronyms and provides little focus on pedagogy or the curriculum, it's time to add some more **E** (Educators) to the mix. If you're pressured to start up with laptops right away, make sure you don't overlook the importance of **P** (Planning) so that you can get it right the first time. While there's no set formula for how much planning should be done, "as much as possible" is always a good yardstick. Finally, it's crucial to keep your focus during the difficult months of planning, setup, and initial roll-out so that you don't let contingency dilute your vision along the way. Inevitably, what separates the successful programs from the less successful is the **C** (Commitment) of leaders. Effective use of technology requires continual planning, ongoing professional development, frequent assessment, and the commitment of resources, including dollars and staff.

Chapter 1
THE PECK SCHOOL

Introduction

WALK THROUGH THE DOUBLE DOORS of the main entrance of The Peck School and you'll find yourself surrounded by beautiful wood paneling decorated with carved moldings from an earlier age. Gaze upward and your eyes will follow an ornate staircase leading to a landing backed by a multicolored, lead-paned, stained glass window. It's the source of the many-hued light that floods the open area below.

To your right is a striking fireplace, with a large painting above it. In fact, paintings hang on every wall, because Peck uses its lobby as an art gallery and displays works by different artists on a rotating basis.

If you walk forward a few steps, you'll notice a small window to your left with a switch next to it. Turn this switch on, bend down to look through the window, and you'll see a scene that looks similar to the room you're standing in. It's filled with tiny furniture. Peer inside and you'll see a miniature knight clad in full armor. You're in an institution that combines tradition and academics with a love of students, a self-termed "family school."

Suddenly, it's 8 a.m. and you hear the opening bell. Boys and girls dressed in uniforms enter through the double doors, rolling or carrying backpacks. There's something different about many of the older students, however. They carry silver briefcases rather than the standard backpack. These are Peck's seventh- and eighth-graders, who are given laptops to use 24/7 for all their schoolwork. Just a few minutes ago, many of them were in the "before school" program—laptops open—studying, printing, and listening to music.

Look around the walls of Peck and you might spot a wireless access device, blinking intermittently, sending a signal for faculty and student laptops. These access points provide a little 21st-century razzle-dazzle to the staid, 19th-century wood paneling.

Figure 1.1
Two students work on their wireless laptops at The Peck School.

TIMELINE
THE PECK SCHOOL'S LAPTOP PROGRAM

1982 ▶	Peck chooses the Apple II as a hardware platform for its wealth of educational software.
September 1984 ▶	Elisabeth Fraser becomes Peck's first technology chair.
September 1985 ▶	Technology teacher hired for the Lower School. Apple computers are used to teach Logo.
October 1993 ▶	2020 Vision document represents a first draft of the Peck School Technology Plan.
May 1994 ▶	20 student laptops are purchased to equip one classroom.
September 1994 ▶	Leslie Maguire hired to be Upper School technology coordinator.
	Board presentation on funding needs for a new seventh- and eighth-grade school building with an infrastructure to support laptops.
	Faculty workshops on word processing and network use.
January 1995 ▶	Board considers whether to require students to purchase their own laptop.
	A Finance Committee report recommends a fundraising effort to provide students with laptops, targeting Grades 5–8.
	Professional Development plan for technology instituted.
May 1995 ▶	First school-wide technology showcase.
September 1995 ▶	New building for Grades 7 and 8 opens for classes.
February 1996 ▶	Updated technology plan refers to "school-owned laptops" or "student-owned laptops."
September 1996 ▶	Eight teacher laptops are purchased to support technology and communications classes.
September 1997 ▶	Upper School academic faculty provided with school-owned laptops, a gift from the Parents Association.
	A technical support specialist is hired.

Founded in 1893, The Peck School is a coed K–8 independent school in Morristown, New Jersey. Known for its academic rigor, Peck attracts students from 37 zip codes. They attend an accelerated educational program that stresses academics, personal responsibility, hard work, athletics, the arts, and technology.

The 2005–2006 school year marks the 7th year that laptops have been provided to every seventh- and eighth-grade student at Peck. All faculty members were given laptops 8 years ago. My predecessor as head of technology at Peck, Elisabeth Fraser, was the visionary and steward for this successful program from its inception in 1998 until I took over in June 2002.

Why Laptops? Why Peck?

The initial goal of the laptop program, Fraser remembers, was to encourage more seamless integration of technology into all aspects of the curriculum. Having tapped into the wisdom of her husband (a scientist and researcher at Bell Labs), Fraser believed that everyone, everywhere, would soon be using laptops. The earlier Peck School students got comfortable with this technology, the better it would be for their educational and career prospects.

Peck had already made significant strides with computers, integrating them into the math curriculum in the 1980s. Two computer labs were outfitted in the early '90s, permitting regular computer classes to be offered. Even with these resources, however, disparities remained between home and school in terms of software and hardware. Peck decided to address this issue by purchasing home and school licenses for AppleWorks, a software suite that can run on both PCs and Macs.

This helped, but it still wasn't enough to ensure uniform and problem-free transportation of work from home to school and back again. Some students didn't have ready access to computers at home. Some had computers or printers in need of repair. In addition, many students who participated in sports often traveled on weekends and were unable to use the family computer to complete assignments. Students whose parents were divorced often split their time between two residences that didn't have the same computer resources. This typically resulted in 10,000 student excuses at homework-collection time, and frustration ensued for the entire staff and faculty.

Enter the portable, affordable laptop. If every student were given an identical laptop computer, the home-to-school connection would be facilitated, travel problems would be mitigated, and homework could be uniformly processed. In addition, technology skill-building could be integrated into the curriculum in a much more consistent and enduring way than was possible before, when students had to travel once or twice a week to the computer lab.

Why did a school steeped in more than 100 years of tradition become one of the earliest to institute a 1-to-1 laptop program? Elisabeth Fraser's leadership was certainly critical, but it also may have to do with the fact that educators at The Peck School tend to be early adopters by nature. A favorable mention of computers is made as early as 1976 in *Because They Cared* (Morrison, 1992), a history of the first 100 years of The Peck School. A student quote from the 1976 yearbook reads: "During the Spring Term, we took a computer course at the Newark Institute of Technology. We learned a lot about how to program a computer and look at problems from different angles" (ibid., p. 81). Even at this early date, educators at Peck recognized the value of computers in the classroom and took the time to send students to a computer institution.

In 1980, four TRS-80 computers were donated by the school's Mother's Association. That same year, computer study was made an official part of the seventh-grade math curriculum. Seven brand-new Apple IIe computers followed for K–8 classes. In 1984, the first computer lab was completed in the Lower School, and a different space was designated for Upper School computers. These computers were used for Logo programming and word processing.

Along with this affinity for computer technology, The Peck School also has a tradition of regularly assessing its curriculum and approach to learning. This is done every 5 years or so in part to prepare for the Middle States and other accreditations, but also because Peck's leaders are committed to pursuing more effective teaching and learning.

TIMELINE
THE PECK SCHOOL'S LAPTOP PROGRAM

September 1998 ▶ All faculty members are provided with school-owned laptops.

September 1998 ▶ A stipend is paid to six teachers to be TAG (Technically Adept Gurus) Team members to support faculty and staff.

Board members visit classrooms to see and participate in laptop learning.

July 1999 ▶ Tech support specialist leaves, new person hired as a systems administrator.

September 1999 ▶ All seventh and eighth grade students are provided with school-owned laptops.

January 2000 ▶ Music Department uses 20 old laptops for MIDI lab and music production.

October 2001 ▶ Tech support person hired to run the laptop program.

June 2002 ▶ Pamela Livingston takes over for retiring Elizabeth Fraser as head of technology.

Peck's laptop program is evaluated by technology directors from Choate Rosemary Hall and Dwight-Englewood School.

June 2005 ▶ Construction begins on Academic Link building and new gym, both fully wireless

September 2005 ▶ Laptops are provided to every sixth grader, but must stay in school on a cart. Laptops are also provide to fifth graders (2-to-1) on a cart.

New schedule begins. Seventh and eighth graders no longer have formal technology classes. Laptops are used throughout classes instead. Fifth and sixth graders continue to take technology classes once every 6 days, with teachers using laptops as part of regular class instruction.

P Is for Planning

Planning a major initiative at The Peck School always involves the Board of Trustees, a group of volunteers—educators, business leaders, and parents—who are mandated to oversee the school's fiscal health and steer the school into the future. The board hires and evaluates the Head of School and provides stewardship over the school's future, ensuring its continuance for future generations.

Peck School is fortunate to have a strong and committed board whose members bring a variety of skills and professional expertise to the table. When Fraser first proposed the idea of a 1-to-1 laptop program, the board was ready to role up its collective sleeves and work with Peck's faculty to make things happen. Cathy Walsh, a Peck board member for 9 years, and a current member of the board's Executive Committee, recalls that the first crucial step was to get everyone on the board up to speed on the unique capabilities of laptops: "I think we knew right away that we had to keep educating everybody. When I joined the board, we found that we had to educate the board before we could educate parents, teachers, or anyone" (personal communication, August 30, 2000).

First, board members visited a technology-infused corporation to see how 1-to-1 access to computers was being managed in a corporate environment and what impact this access was having on employee productivity and interoffice communication. They took a virtual tour of the building and realized how 1-to-1 access could be used in the classroom for, say, halving a sphere to understand its volume. Since many board members came from corporations and industry, and because few 1-to-1 school programs existed at that time, they also toured a high tech company. These visits gave them a better idea of how technology skill development could benefit Peck School students.

Not everyone was immediately convinced that putting laptops into the hands of every seventh- and eighth-grade student made sense for the school, either educationally, philosophically, or fiscally. But once board members were able to see 1-to-1 in action and it was no longer just a concept in their minds, things started to happen.

First, the board nominated one of its members to co-chair the Technology Committee with Walsh. Together, the two co-chairs devised a strategy of reaching out to all stakeholders to solicit their buy-in (**E** for educators), asking them to contribute ideas and assess current capacity and progress (**P** for planning). Through their efforts, the 1-to-1 laptop initiative stayed alive and fresh in the minds of faculty and staff, encouraging their active support (**C** for commitment).

Their approach to consensus-building is an exemplar of how to get multiple stakeholders educated, informed, and on board. A number of presentations featuring laptops were arranged, and faculty and staff members were regularly asked to share their feelings and concerns. Teachers and administrators formed groups and committees to reflect on the potential and challenges of implementing a laptop program. They discussed the educational and logistical pros and cons and imagined what could be done in the future. Educators (**E**) were centrally involved in the entire process.

Information about the initiative's ongoing progress was shared with the entire school community through official communications from Peck's Head of School, David Frothingham; Elisabeth Fraser's internal communiqués; the Peck Tech News newsletter (filled with articles from students, parents, administrators, teachers, and board members);

letters home to parents; and the publication of a thoroughly revised and detailed technology plan for the school. No one could feel that details weren't forthcoming or that people weren't working hard to inform them. The education of stakeholders was vital, ongoing, and varied in its delivery.

Peck also sought out exemplars to help in planning (**P**) its program. Committee members researched the Anytime, Anywhere Learning (AAL) program and its group of 52 schools, as well as Cincinnati Country Day School's formalized laptop institute for schools. The AAL program was the focus of a 3-year study by the independent research group Rockman *et al*, which provided invaluable information on the benefits and challenges these early adopter schools encountered. Cincinnati Country Day School provided ideas on planning, implementing, managing, and sustaining a laptop program. In addition, they hosted a visit by several Peck faculty and board members.

Paying for It

Independent schools such as Peck rely on tuition, donations, and grants to run the school. Adding a major program to the school's budget isn't done without considerable thought and planning. Walsh remembers that funding was an issue which generated a lot of discussion during the planning stages. One early funding suggestion was the institution of a dedicated technology fee or laptop fee. However, Peck had never before levied any separate book or athletic fees, relying instead on a single yearly tuition fee to cover the majority of costs. With that as a precedent, the board decided to raise tuition to cover the first-year cost of laptops. That higher tuition rate has been retained in subsequent years, sustaining the program year after year.

While this raise in tuition was used to pay for laptops, the board decided to pay for other, related costs—primarily to upgrade the school's network and infrastructure—by inaugurating a small capital campaign. Typically, capital campaigns at independent schools are fundraisers for specific improvements or programs. This campaign was called Challenge 2000, and a target of $650,000 was set. A committee went to work to ask for contributions from board members, parents, alumni, faculty, and others affiliated with the school. A special effort was made to solicit those parents whose children were scheduled to get the laptops in the first and second years, since they would receive the most immediate benefits. In the end, enough money was raised to pay for the laptops and the infrastructural improvements needed to support them, and a laptop program was born.

Staffing

The talent and expertise of the computer coordinators at Peck—Leslie Maguire for the Upper School (Grades 5–8) and Theresa Deehan for the Lower School (Grades K–4)—have from the beginning been critical to the planning and implementation of the laptop program. Visitors to Peck School often remark on the school's commitment (**C**) to technology in general and the laptop program in particular, and much of the credit goes to these technology professionals.

Peck also decided to hire another full-time technology support person for the laptop program. The school realized that if laptops were to be truly integrated into everyday learning tasks, they would have to be maintained and repaired on a timely basis so that teachers and students could rely on them. Any sustained downtime could lead to potentially devastating effects on the seventh- and eighth-grade curriculum. So having a dedicated tech support staff to handle setup, configuration, distribution, and maintenance was deemed critical to the long-term success of the program.

Peck currently has two excellent, service-oriented tech support people on staff: Kevin Grieshaber, network manager, and Nirav Patel, technical support specialist. Both hold multiple technical certifications in hardware, software, and network administration, and both are genuinely kind and helpful. When the person who comes to fix a teacher's misbehaving laptop is pleasant, efficient, competent, and never condescending, teachers are more likely to have a positive view of the role technology can play in their classrooms.

A First Step Toward 24/7—Rolling Carts

Having your own laptop to use 24/7 is a serious responsibility, one that 12-year-old students aren't always ready to handle. Consequently, laptops are provided to fifth- and sixth-graders on rolling carts and are to be used in classrooms only. Fifth-graders share laptops 2-to-1: two students are assigned one laptop that can be used for teacher-directed activities. The rolling carts we use are "wet carts," meaning they're wired to provide electrical charging for the laptops.

Figure 1.2
Laptops plugged into a rolling cart.

Because Peck has only two homerooms per grade, two students to a laptop doesn't cause much contention. Classes for all subjects are split into groups of 18 students, so fifth-grade teachers arrange their use of laptops around class meeting times. Usually, when one homeroom needs the laptops, the other homeroom doesn't. In addition, technology classes that teach technology skills using content from the academic subjects are held regularly. These classes also emphasize laptop care and use.

Starting in 2005, all sixth-grade students were given 1-to-1 access to laptops on a rolling cart for use on teacher-directed projects and activities. Formal technology classes for sixth-graders reinforce basic technology skills, including the care and use of laptops. As in fifth grade, sixth-grade technology classes incorporate content from academic subjects.

Laptops are used frequently to support the curriculum for fifth- and sixth-grade English, history, math, science, and language arts. In addition, several new "short course" offerings—such as iMovie, PowerPoint and public speaking, Adobe Photoshop Elements, and Earthquake Research—make regular use of laptops. Fifth- and sixth-grade students can check their homework assignments online using FirstClass software, and participate in regular homework conferences on every subject that they can access from school or at home. Parents can check their children's homework in this way as well.

Tech Support

Peck leaders who planned the laptop program realized their commitment (**C**) to success would require a full-time tech support specialist to help the network manager manage the new hardware.

A major part of the specialist's job is care of the laptops and first-line support to students and teachers who have computer issues. Students bring their laptop issues to the tech support area during recess, before and after school, and sometimes during school. Problems include logic board failures, screen problems, lost or forgotten power cords, and setup issues related to different networking configurations at home and at school.

Figure 1.3
Tools of the trade at Peck: spare and loaner parts.

We keep a ready supply of extra power cords and batteries and help students with their dial-up, DSL, or cable modem connections so that they can access their home Internet accounts. We've arranged with Apple Computer to help us with timely repair and replacement of defective or damaged laptops. Apple determines if the iBook needs repair because of normal wear and tear, hardware failure (covered by our extended warranty), or user damage. If the problem is due to damage, we share the cost of repairing the unit with the student's parents.

Thanks to our technical support staff's skills and their genuine desire to help, we've had relatively little difficulty integrating laptops into the daily routine at The Peck School. Tech staff members are always available via walkie-talkies and are quick to come to the aid of teachers and students when failures or problems occur.

They've also helped us resolve bigger issues, such as the difficulties we experienced in 2002 when we installed a wireless network. The initial placement of wireless access points around the school wasn't always the best; there were dead zones in some areas and signal interference in others. Tech support resolved these issues by walking around the school with laptops and redesigning access point placement. Our network coverage is now solid. As part of our new building construction, we've also upgraded some of our older wireless access points to Cisco equipment and have hired a systems integrator to plan a wireless infrastructure for our entire campus.

Network Infrastructure

As with many schools, Peck's original network was installed in the early '90s. It was an Ethernet network, with cabling designed to support desktop computers in classrooms and computer labs. For the most part, this meant small hubs able to accommodate several computers in a single classroom location. Computers had to be placed close enough to the hubs to connect their network cards to the hub port. Some of these hubs are still in place in Peck's Lower School, where laptops aren't used.

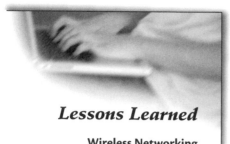

Lessons Learned

Wireless Networking and Hindsight

Planning for a 1-to-1 laptop program in today's schools means planning for wireless access. You need enough electrical outlets and access points around the school to provide wireless network coverage for everyone. Wireless access still requires an Ethernet backbone, however, because behind every wireless access station is an Ethernet port and cable. Wireless works from the wall outward, but cables still need to be pulled through the walls and ceilings. Electricity still needs to be provided at access points unless power is fed to them directly by the network switches.

Peck benefited from having a parent who worked for the Lucent Corporation, which provided network hardware and wiring at a reduced cost. The network hardware was originally leased for 3 years to allow the technology department to replace it with better, faster equipment when it became available. Much of that equipment has since been replaced, but the item that cost the most—wiring—is still in use 8 years later.

All computer networks need continual maintenance and updating, and the network that supports Peck's laptop program has changed considerably since the laptops were first introduced. Among other things, Cisco switches have replaced older, unmanaged ones. Also, an SMTP gateway with Web filtering has been brought online, and industrial-strength antivirus and firewall capabilities have been installed on a new server that replaced the original Unix box. In the next year, Peck will be performing a wireless access evaluation and plan as an extension of new construction to be completed in September 2006.

Networks are continually morphing entities. Once state-of-the-art 10 Mbps Ethernet networks first gave way to 100 Mbps Ethernet and then to gigabit Ethernet. T1 lines have given way to T3 lines. Switches and connections need periodic upgrading, as do firewalls, packet shaping devices... the list goes on and on. At The Peck School, our best defense has been a network manager who has stayed on top of developments and vendors who have taken the time to understand our plans and ideas for growth.

See chapters 5 and 7 for ways to keep your network running smoothly, even with the demands placed on it by a 1-to-1 program.

Building Design

The timing of the 1-to-1 laptop initiative was very fortunate because it coincided with the design and construction of a new building at The Peck School. The best time to install network cables is before walls are completed so that you don't have to cut through Sheetrock or other materials. Similarly, the best time to institute a laptop program is during the construction of a new building, when planners are designing classrooms, storage for students, network cabling, and so forth. For Peck, this meant that all electrical and network connections were planned, purchased, and installed with the needs of the laptop program in mind. Many districts and schools face the challenge of retrofitting their buildings for laptops, but Peck could literally begin from the ground up and design a building around, and for, laptops.

There did turn out to be one need for retrofitting, however. The building was finished and in use when the technology department realized the soft-sided cases originally purchased for the laptops were providing too little protection. Rather than install lockers, which are too narrow for laptops and hard-sided cases, Peck decided to build open, square cubbies, with anchor bolts for long, looping cables. At the ends of each cable are loops through which a regular Master combination lock can be threaded.

Figure 1.4
Peck School's cubbies accommodate laptops locked in place.

Students lock their laptops in these cubbies by threading the cables through the handles of the hard-sided cases and closing the combination lock (see Figure 1.4). In this way, laptops can be secured when not in use. Teachers check the laptops frequently to be sure they're all locked in place; if not, they're "kidnapped" and brought to the Upper School office. Students face disciplinary action if they fail to secure their laptop properly. Cubbies have been such an effective addition to the seventh- and eighth-grade building that Peck's new Academic Link building (under construction) will have cubbies as well.

Even though the CT building (for seventh- and eighth-graders) was designed for laptops, it wasn't originally designed for a wireless network. In fact, although some of the design features made sense when the building was constructed 10 years ago, they aren't used much anymore. For instance, in the multipurpose room, pull-down electrical outlets were installed in the ceiling so that students could plug in their laptops. These are rarely used now, because iBook batteries last longer. In the new Academic Link building under construction, this design feature has been replaced by floor boxes housing both electrical and data outlets.

The long tables with hard-wired Ethernet drops in place that were purchased especially for the CT building are another example. Students originally used Ethernet cables to plug their laptops into the tables, which also had electrical outlets. These tables have since been moved to storage because network access is fully wireless and most students arrive at school with fully charged batteries.

While a few overhead projectors were included in the original design, we've since added several more. We're planning to install overhead projectors in every classroom in our new buildings as well. Some in the new building will be wireless, and some will have hard-wired connections for laptops or desktops.

Protective Cases

Peck initially purchased soft-sided, briefcase-like cases for its laptops. Within the first year, however, many laptops suffered major damage, particularly to their screens. The cost to repair them was often greater than the cost of a new computer. These cases just weren't standing up to the wear and tear that seventh- and eighth-graders were putting their laptops through while transporting them to and from school in the back of a car. They were no doubt surrounded by hockey equipment, tennis rackets, backpacks full of books, and maybe a golden retriever or two.

Cautionary Tale

Laptop Cases

Peck initially used soft-sided laptop cases and experienced major damage, particularly to screens. Moving to hard-sided cases cut damage costs by more than half. Samsonite makes an aluminum case with a combination lock that works perfectly for Peck's needs, especially since a local luggage company was willing to customize the cases' interior foam padding to fit the iBook laptops that Peck students were using.

After investigating other options, Peck decided to purchase Zero Halliburton cases, which are exceedingly sturdy. These have proven to be equal to everything that Peck School seventh- and eighth-graders have (quite literally) thrown at them. There's even a tale, which fortunately has neither been confirmed nor repeated, about an SUV running over a case without damaging the laptop inside. In 2003, Peck contracted with a local luggage store to purchase hard-sided Samsonite cases that were nearly as durable but cost much less. The store customized the cases by cutting the interior foam padding in the shape of an iBook. These cases, which cost $165 apiece, have worked extremely well to protect the school's investment in technology. So far, the only damage that has occurred has happened when the laptops have been outside of the case.

The school has also looked at various "always-on" protective case options such as those from InfoCase, and Peck may go in that direction in the future. However, since the cases open easily and the laptop could slip out, these cases may not fit so easily into Peck's cubbie and cable-lock system. The school will revisit this issue annually as more cases and options become available.

Insurance

For the first several years of the laptop program, insurance was purchased from a company that specialized in insuring laptops for schools. The premium was high, about $12,000 per year for the 80 laptops. This policy covered all damages over and above Apple's extended warranty, less a $100 deductible. If the damage occurred because of neglect or abuse, the school submitted the bill to the insurance company, received a check, and billed the parents for the deductible. This worked well, especially before more durable cases were purchased for each laptop.

Once the school purchased hard-shell protective cases, however, damage to the laptops began to occur much less frequently. Administrators reviewed the insurance policy and realized that for Peck's annual $12,000 payment, the school was receiving less than $2,000 back for damaged equipment. Most problems were being covered by Apple's extended warranty, and damage wasn't excessive. To date, fortunately, there's been no incidence of theft. Consequently, the decision was made to become self-insured and cover the cost of laptop damage directly.

When Apple determines damage is over and above the warranty plan in place, Peck School splits the cost of the damage with parents of students who incur the damage. Generally, the most costly damage is to laptop screens, which can cost $900 to repair or replace. So far, it's been cheaper to self-insure, since generally only three or four such incidents occur per year.

The Peck School laptop program is small enough for this plan to work. Other schools and districts will have to seriously consider whether this plan makes sense for them. Every year, Peck looks at these costs and determines how much they're impacting the budget, and so far the decision to self-insure has proved cost-effective.

Professional Development and Teacher Support

Peck knew that for technology to be integrated successfully into the classroom, teachers had to be on board with the program first. To facilitate this, teachers were given laptops a full year before students. In addition, several professional development initiatives were begun to support teachers' use of the laptops in their everyday teaching and preparation.

One initiative was known as the TAG Team approach. Technology-Adept Gurus— faculty members who already had an affinity for computers and were willing to be trained a bit more—were identified to provide peer-level technical support to other teachers. A special stipend was given to these TAG teachers. This initiative was based on the premise that it's often less intimidating to ask a colleague for help than it is to call technical support.

Figure 1.5
Inspiration created by Peck School's Leslie Maguire, Upper School technology coordinator, showing how teachers were brought on board with the laptop program.

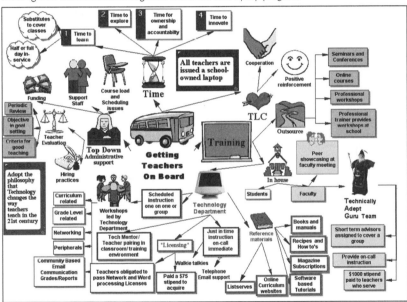

Another initiative was "licensing" teachers for their demonstrated ability to use the network and productivity software. Teachers who attended a series of classes and passed a battery of skills tests earned a license when they were finished. It carried a small stipend as well as a certificate of completion.

These classes were conducted using differentiated instruction principles. Three types of training were offered. The first involved a tech-trainer-led computer lab, where teachers followed instructions step-by-step to familiarize themselves with a particular program or process. A second type brought teachers together to learn with a self-guided handout, with the tech trainer circulating to answer questions and fix glitches. The third approach was entirely do-it-yourself. These different training methods were supplemented and reinforced at regular faculty meetings. Teacher projects and technology successes were showcased, and teachers were able to ask questions and learn from one another.

A commitment to just-in-time learning and just-in-time technical support was part of the plan from the beginning. When teachers need to learn or use something new, they know the technology department will respond quickly to phone or e-mail requests, arriving within minutes to get them out of a jam. This technical support helps feed professional development, since Peck's network manager and tech support specialist always discuss with teachers what they're doing to fix the problem. Then, they show them how to do it the next time themselves.

One Teacher Tells His Story: Don Diebold

Without educators (**E**) in the classroom who truly believe in the potential of laptops to transform the learning environment, and without their commitment (**C**) and willingness to change their teaching approaches to embrace this new technology, the laptop program at The Peck School would not have flourished as it has for the past 8 years.

Figure 1.6
Don Diebold is committed to improving teaching processes through the use of technology.

One of these committed teachers and leaders, Don Diebold, typifies the experience many teachers have gone through over the years while adopting and embracing computer technology.

Diebold has taught at Peck for 33 years. He's Peck's athletic director and teaches all seventh- and eighth-grade science classes. When he came to Peck in 1973, he was immediately impressed with how the administration promoted creativity in the classroom, not just in the curriculum but also in the mode of instructional delivery. When computer technology started to take hold in the corporate world, he paid close attention, knowing instinctively that the same technology would eventually find its way to the classroom.

Diebold saw how technology was helping corporations accomplish tasks more efficiently, so he began using technology to automate the athletic department. He remembers first using word processing and spreadsheet programs to inventory equipment and uniforms. Previously, as changes occurred, schedules and inventories had to be typed, crossed out, and retyped many times. The advantages of doing this work on a computer, including instant access to information and the ability to change details easily, were immediately apparent to him as an administrator.

Seeing how computers could facilitate the running of the athletic department, Diebold began using them to generate tests and lesson plans. However, there wasn't much in the way of digital teaching materials for a number of years. When the World Wide Web got off the ground in the early '90s and software and hardware options for science teaching and laboratory work became more widely available, he realized it would just be a matter of time till these professional science applications began to filter into the classroom.

Next came laptops on a rolling cart. Diebold requested and received special hardware and software to collect data for seventh- and eighth-grade science labs. The result was higher quality lab reports, which took less time for students to complete and teachers to assess. Whereas 90% of lab time had formerly been spent on mechanics and paperwork, and only 10% on working with students to deepen their conceptual approach to assignments, Diebold now found he could spend "a bigger percentage of time on teaching students how to think like a scientist and less time on the mechanics of the process" (personal interview, October 6, 2005).

What he describes is exactly what an outside evaluator picked up on very quickly when he visited Diebold's class in December 2002. Joel Backon, director of information technology at another independent school, Choate Rosemary Hall, visited Peck that year in response to Peck's request for an outside evaluation of its laptop program. In his report, Backon singled out Diebold's use of laptops in the science lab for particular praise (ibid.):

> In your science program, Mr. Diebold's observations that the use of laptops and probes for scientific investigation has improved the quality of lab reports and increased the number and complexity of labs is evidence that technology integration is working. Many high school teachers find these notions counterintuitive. Because you are integrating rather than simply using technology, you have captured additional class time rather than sacrificing it.

As technology has gotten better, Diebold's classes have become more integrated. He's been able to find more and better teaching resources, and laptops have become faster, more reliable, and easier to use. The Internet has provided him with useful professional contacts: for example, a professor at the University of Virginia who had developed dissection software was willing to work with Diebold to give him a better understanding of how it worked and what its benefits were.

The Web also provides numerous learning opportunities for his seventh- and eighth-grade students. Diebold reports: "I have Web sites for every concept I teach. Some are simple sites that are easy to understand, others are more complex ones that I use just for the graphics" (ibid.). The value of the Web for him is how rapidly it responds to changing ideas about science.

Before Peck School started its laptop program, Diebold says, "there was a lot of debate between the board, the administration, and the faculty as to whether [laptop use] was appropriate. The users of laptops did presentations to the board on numerous occasions to show how laptops could be used. It worked because of the vision of administration, trustees, and the head of technology at that time, as well as some of us in the faculty who believed technology was crucial to education in the future" (ibid.). While cautioning that "traditional methods are still needed—nothing replaces the teacher" (ibid.), Diebold believes that technology can help teachers communicate their passion for learning to a new generation of students more comfortable with computers and the Internet than with thick reference books.

Diebold tries to incorporate laptops into everything he does in class. He e-mails lesson plans to his students ahead of time to inform them before the class meets. Student assignments are returned by e-mail so that an electronic backup copy of all student work exists. Diebold is enthusiastic about the changes to his teaching process that the laptops have helped bring about, particularly in their ability to support differentiated instruction. He says (ibid.):

> I cover the same concepts that I did prior to the laptops but I do so in probably 200% greater depth than I did before. The laptops enable me to conduct a class where I guide the students, spend more time with those having difficulty with fundamental concepts or skills, and allow other students to move forward with enrichment work related to what we are studying. I can reach every student in the classroom. The laptops have allowed me to do that without doing double the work... We need to find as many different ways as possible to say the same things. That is what a master teacher can do with technology: show concepts in many different ways, and be ready with a mode of delivery that works for every student, no matter where they are developmentally.

The relative strengths of every student can be encouraged with a laptop, Diebold believes. The creative student may create a poster or a PowerPoint presentation to explain a scientific concept with artistic flair, while the analytical student may feel more comfortable explaining the same concept with a chart generated from a spreadsheet program. The fact that laptops can support both students' strengths inspires their passion for learning.

Diebold believes that teachers need to act now to embrace technology, because that increasingly is the language students speak: "Technology is their language. It's a huge part of their lives, of the world they are living in today. If you don't talk their language you are not going to reach them" (ibid.). He is committed (**C**) to Peck's laptop program because it puts students first and gives them the best tools available to organize and personalize their learning. This is why it works.

Acceptable Use and Parent Buy-In

After much discussion and nearly going another direction, Peck decided to raise its tuition and provide laptops to all seventh- and eight-grade students as part of the tuition cost. This was in lieu of charging an extra laptop fee or asking parents to buy the laptops on their own.

It's true that Peck has a graduated tuition, with parents of seventh- and eighth-graders paying higher tuition. But when the tuition increase for the laptop program was instituted, it was decided to make it an across-the-board increase that would be shared by all constituents. The idea was that younger students will eventually benefit from the laptops and that Peck's overall technology program builds from kindergarten right up to the eighth grade, providing a solid base for effective laptop use.

This approach answered the concern of many parents about having to pay extra money. It also allowed Peck to retain ownership of the computers, simplifying software compatibility, maintenance, and other issues. Still, there was then, as there is now, a need to reach out to parents to solicit their buy-in and support for the 1-to-1 laptop program. As a consequence, parental outreach and education are crucial to the program's ongoing success.

Every year, parents are sent information about the program, and all seventh-grade parents purchase a case for the laptop. The parent handbook has a special section on laptop use and maintenance, which is updated every summer (see appendix A). In addition, the Peck School Acceptable Use Policy (also in appendix A) must be signed every year by the parent(s) or guardian(s), as well as by the student. Finally, parents must also sign a laptop assessment sheet every year that details the serial number and the condition of the laptop.

This document contains a statement that outlines parental responsibility for the costs of any damages not covered by the laptop warranty.

Since Peck wants students to use their laptops in meaningful and appropriate ways, the Peck School Acceptable Use Policy has a student summary which requires that all use of computers be **LARK**.

The **L** stands for **legal**, which covers plagiarism issues as well as the downloading of unpurchased music and software. Recently, in a "themes" class for seventh-graders, teachers divided classes in half and asked each half to investigate Napster vs. Metallica, a file-sharing case of several years back. The students themselves came to the conclusion that copying music onto a CD and distributing it to friends is illegal.

The **A** is for **appropriate**. Seventh-graders are told that this refers not only to the sophisticated 13-year-old's view of whether material is appropriate, but also to what the student's grandmother, 4-year old sister, and Peck School teachers and administrators would consider appropriate. This approach works better for students and helps them step outside their own norms.

R stands for **responsible**. Responsible care and use includes not having a can of Coca-Cola next to the computer, and not balancing the laptop precariously on one's knees while sitting on a cement sidewalk.

Cautionary Tale

Having LARK Is Not Enough

Having LARK as your acceptable use policy doesn't preclude correction, discipline, and monitoring. Students at Peck are told that their laptops, e-mail accounts, and network use are not private but subject to oversight and inspection. However, student infractions are generally handled as teachable moments. They're considered opportunities for students to reflect on their actions both in light of LARK and in terms of their own reputations and membership in a community of learners.

Finally, **K** is for **kind**. Peck is committed to being a community of people who are caring and kind to one another, and this must be exhibited in computer use as well. Every use of computers needs to be kind, from e-mail messages, to pictures and images chosen for display, to respect for passwords and personal files.

Overall, these methods have worked very smoothly. According to Cathy Walsh, during the first year of the program one parent said she didn't want her child to receive a laptop. Walsh solved that by telling her she'd already paid for it and described how tuition includes a laptop. Today, most parents sending their children to Peck know all about its technology program, and Peck's admissions director makes sure that prospective parents tour classrooms with laptops and learn about the school's plan to go to a fully wireless campus. The laptop program has become a major factor in encouraging parents to consider The Peck School.

Laptop Integration

Peck's goal from the very beginning of the 1-to-1 laptop program has been to integrate these digital assistants as much as possible into daily classroom activities. Wherever appropriate, laptops have become a part of seventh- and eighth-grade teaching, learning, communicating, thinking, and problem solving. This process of integration is repeated

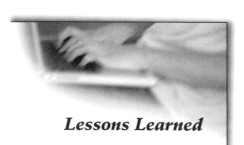

Lessons Learned

Permission Forms

Sending a student home with a shiny new laptop computer and a set of forms for the student and parent to sign doesn't mean the forms will necessarily come back the next day. Or the day after. Or even the next month! To combat this problem, The Peck School requires that both the forms and the computer be returned the next day. If the forms haven't been signed, the student doesn't get the shiny new laptop back, and instead gets an old, slow, ugly loaner computer to use. Since every student naturally wants the beautiful, fast iBook and will do whatever it takes to keep it, few forget to bring their signed forms back on a timely basis.

day in and day out, and teachers, students, and parents have learned to accept the process that this integration requires.

It isn't always easy.

It requires that educators commit to continually evaluating laptop use in their classrooms. Every day, teachers must address the management challenges presented by classrooms of laptop-enabled adolescents. They must regularly check out new online textbooks and resources and stay current with education technology developments and approaches.

It requires an administration willing to invest the resources and time needed to make sure the program continues and flourishes. In Peck's case, this has meant continuous investment in cabling, wireless access points, server rooms, air conditioners, and other infrastructure needs—not just in existing buildings but in every building planned for the future.

It also requires a board of trustees that understands the fiscal responsibility of maintaining an adequate technology budget, approving new technology infrastructure purchases, and staffing the school with experienced technology administrators and tech-savvy teachers.

Integration requires the coordination of all these different pieces, but where it finally plays out is in the classroom, with the integration of the technology into the seventh- and eighth-grade curriculum. Curricular integration requires that teachers help their students get up to speed fast on the hardware features and software applications they'll use the most to get their schoolwork done.

Since the laptop program's inception, Peck has continually addressed the "chicken or egg" debate over whether it's best to teach technology skills as a discrete subject or implicitly, by means of projects. In the next two chapters, you'll read about some schools that have chosen the projects approach, believing that students learn technology skills best in the context of real work.

Peck, however, feels that basic technology skills are very important. We've revamped some of our curriculum to ensure that students spend time learning typing skills (Mavis Beacon, Typing Tutor, Type to Learn) and such basic tasks as printing documents and saving and backing up files to the network. Students also receive training in productivity software (Microsoft Word, Microsoft Excel), concept mapping software (Inspiration), presentation software (MS PowerPoint, TimeLiner), digital editing software (Adobe Photoshop, iMovie), and subject-specific software such as Geometer's Sketchpad. As much as possible, these skills classes use content from the existing academic curriculum.

Program Evaluation

Peck has a long history of evaluating its various programs, and technology is always part of that evaluation. Self-assessment studies are conducted every 5 to 7 years, both to prepare for formal accreditation review and to evaluate the education that students are receiving. Other evaluations are periodically undertaken as well. In 2003, Peck conducted an "Outcomes" evaluation during which Peck graduates, former parents, and former faculty were polled on how well they felt Peck's education measured up after several years.

In December 2002, I requested through my membership in edACCESS (Educational Administrative and Campus Computing Environment at Small Schools, an organization for technology in small independent K–12 schools and colleges) that a team of technology professionals come to Peck to evaluate our laptop program. I was asked by edACCESS to specify a few questions and particular areas for evaluation. edACCESS sent two evaluators, who spent a day with our seventh- and eighth-grade students and teachers. Their subsequent evaluation report was interesting and affirming.

To the question *"Does our technology curriculum and laptop use prepare our students for the ninth grade at rigorous schools?"* Joel Backon, director of information technology at Choate Rosemary Hall, replied (personal communication, June 21, 2003):

> Quantity of content has not traditionally fit well with technology integration...[however,] you have developed an enlightened approach to teaching and learning...[and] your best students could not be more prepared for the most rigorous schools. They will have received an excellent middle school education supplemented by a rich technology experience and the responsibility of managing their studies with a laptop computer—an impressive set of skills and talents for any rising ninth-grader.

Backon also challenged us to move ahead (ibid.), and this became a piece that we added to our "Outcomes" evaluation:

> Think more about outcomes; what you observe and what you expect. How is technology impacting those outcomes? Are you able to develop metrics that will "prove" that you are graduating better students than you graduated ten years ago? Are you able to show that Peck students are more prepared for high school than students at your peer schools?

Peck is currently conducting technology curriculum evaluations, which will be completed after this book goes to press. These evaluations, along with student and teacher surveys conducted every few years, help keep Peck grounded and committed to growth and renewal. Suggestions from evaluators often lead directly to improvements in programs and processes. For instance, one recent reviewer mentioned how frustrated students were with the laptop loaners given out to students who had lost or damaged their iBook. The Technology Department subsequently found that it could provide a slighter better loaner model for basically the same price. This still provided the disincentive of not being as cool and fast as the standard iBooks, without causing as much student frustration.

Figure 1.7
Components of successful laptop programs.

COMPONENTS OF SUCCESSFUL LAPTOP PROGRAMS

Vision
Laptops for students as part of a school improvement plan

Clarity
Communicate, facilitate, and elucidate directly, clearly, and continually

Leadership
Administration and all leaders keep laptops as a front-burner issue, continually removing obstacles

Communication
Plan and goals are communicated to all stakeholders: teachers, administrators, parents, students, board members; Consensus building

Implementation
Teachers have taken workshops and been given laptops; Staffing is addressed; Logistics and network are ready

Purpose
Return to the reason for laptops continually when sticking points occur

Support
Teachers, students, and parents are supported and encouraged; Tech support, classroom support, resource support

Assessment
Every year see how it went and how it's going; Compare to the plan—adapt, adjust, and assess

Conclusion

Over the past 8 years, The Peck School has learned that an academically rigorous and traditional school with an accelerated program can successfully integrate technology into teaching and learning, benefiting both students and teachers alike. Often people think that 1-to-1 is all about replacing traditional pedagogy and rigor with project-based learning and other constructivist practices. While 1-to-1 certainly *can* support this move to more progressive approaches, it can also sustain a traditional program such as Peck's. When students are empowered by 24/7 access to a digital assistant, all the learning they do, both at school and at home, is enhanced.

The next two chapters profile other schools and districts that have implemented 1-to-1 programs. Several of these programs feature a more progressive approach to education. Regardless of the pedagogical philosophy of these different schools, however, what has determined their level of success has been the same: informed educators (**E**) who have taken the time to plan (**P**) their program carefully, and have worked through the implementation challenges and processes with commitment (**C**) and passion.

Chapter 2
INDIVIDUAL SCHOOL PROGRAMS

Introduction

REGARDLESS OF A SCHOOL'S SIZE, population, or technology infrastructure, starting a 1-to-1 program is a major undertaking. In the previous chapter, we looked at the development of The Peck School's laptop program from its earliest planning stages to its current, evolving state. It's a development process made possible by educators' commitment to plan, fund, evaluate, and improve the program year by year. A 1-to-1 program is never a "do it once and you're done" proposition.

For Peck, the commitment to 1-to-1 has had a lot to do with academics: the need to support and sustain students' work, both at school and at home, as well as the desire to integrate technology across all disciplines. All schools considering a laptop initiative will go through similar processes, even though the reasons, contexts, and outcomes may differ depending on the school's composition, mission, and instructional philosophy. In this chapter, we'll look at three other schools that have implemented a 1-to-1 program and see how the same basic ingredients have created distinct but equally successful programs.

The Urban School (www.urbanschool.org) is a high school in San Francisco that's added 1-to-1 laptops to its student-centered learning environment, greatly benefiting students and teachers alike. The school has used laptops to help its students reach out and interact with the community at large, especially with its Telling Their Stories digital storytelling project. Laptops are fully integrated into the curriculum at The Urban School, where computer skills are honed through content-based activities and projects rather than separate computer skills classes. Howard Levin, director of technology, gave generously of his time to contribute to this profile of Urban's award-winning laptop program.

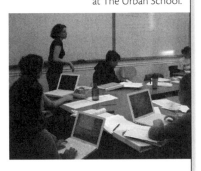

Figure 2.1
A normal day in a normal classroom at The Urban School.

Whitfield School, an independent school in St. Louis that only recently instituted a 1-to-1 program, has found a great deal of immediate success with laptops. Whitfield espouses a process-oriented instructional philosophy, in which the process of learning and not just the content being learned is a primary focus. Alex Inman, Whitfield's technology directory, came to St. Louis a couple of years ago after successfully leading laptop implementation at University Lake School in Milwaukee, Wisconsin. He found a ready and willing constituency at Whitfield School, where educators were already committed to teaching in a student-centered way that is perfectly complemented by ubiquitous computer access.

The Denver School of Science and Technology (DSST) sprang up as a charter school formed and funded with the help of Colorado governor Bill Owens and Microsoft cofounder and chairman Bill Gates. As a brand-new school, DSST was built from the ground up with wireless laptops in mind. Unlike Peck, Urban, and Whitfield, there's been no need to retrofit the curriculum or school infrastructure—or to solicit buy-in from teachers and staff—to make 1-to-1 work at DSST. When technology is such a primary focus of a school's mission and approach that it's included in the school's name, educators know that integrating technology into everything they do is a mandate, not simply a goal.

FUNDING OPTIONS FOR 1-TO-1 PROGRAMS

All 1-to-1 programs are different, taking their particular forms from the populations they serve and the instructional philosophies they embrace. The approaches to funding those programs can be even more unique. There's no perfect or tried-and-true formula for funding a laptop program.

At The Peck School, startup costs were funded by a capital campaign to raise dollars specifically for technology. The program has been sustained in the years since by an across-the-board tuition increase.

At The Urban School, on the other hand, a survey taken of all current and prospective parents showed that most had already planned to buy a laptop for their children. So Urban sold those parents on the idea of paying the school to purchase laptops instead, thereby reaping the economy of scale benefits of a bulk purchase and support package.

Whitfield has phased in their laptop program gradually, limiting it initially to certain grades and providing laptops to teachers first to give them time to create curricular plans. Consequently, Whitfield is now funding its programs from existing dollars.

The Denver School of Science and Technology, a charter school, has received grants and funding from many sources to run its state-of-the-art wireless laptop program.

The Urban School, San Francisco

The Urban School in San Francisco is an independent coed high school with 265 students in Grades 9 through 12. Administrators plan to grow the school to about 320 students in the next few years and add a building in response to the increasing competition in San Francisco for private school space.

The Urban School prides itself on its student-centered philosophy and has received awards for its student-generated digital storytelling program titled Telling Their Stories: An Oral History Archive (www.tellingstories.org). With compelling interviews and profiles of Holocaust survivors, as well as concentration camp liberators and Japanese-American internees, this excellent program is an exemplary model of project-based learning that integrates technology and speaks to audiences far beyond the classroom.

Director of Technology Howard Levin relates that some of the biggest successes of Urban's laptop program—in place since 2000—have come in the most surprising areas. For example, teachers in the language arts program were among the most hesitant and unconvinced of faculty members when the program began, but they're now among its strongest supporters. This difference in attitude, Levin says, is the result of those teachers "finding [laptop] tools that enhanced their ability to engage students in serious discussion."

Teachers at The Urban School were first given laptops in 2000, and laptops for students were provided on mobile carts. This didn't prove to be the best for students, however, and Levin now believes that students should have been given their own laptops from the beginning. The biggest initial challenge was simply getting the program started. At first, faculty members didn't express a lot of interest; the majority of teachers seemed rather ambivalent about the laptop program, seeing it as more of a nuisance than a benefit. Fortunately, most went along with it without too much resistance. The few individuals who strongly opposed the program did not, in the end, stand in the way of implementation.

Today, faculty members are nearly unanimous in their strong approval of the laptop program, and Urban's biggest challenge is simply keeping up with laptop maintenance issues. When laptops are totally integrated into a school curriculum, all school assignments involve them, and timely repair and maintenance become crucial to learning outcomes. "If [students] lose the laptop for 15 minutes," Levin says, "that can be devastating." Managing the human resources needed to support the program has become Levin's No. 1 job.

GETTING TEACHERS ON BOARD

It took 3 or 4 years for Urban School to go from the initial laptop program proposal to final implementation. It was first announced in 1998 as a single line in the school's strategic plan. Head of School Mark Salkind wanted to institute the laptop program, and he hired Levin to help pull it off. To pave the way among faculty members, Levin led a series of technology workshops offered over several summers. These workshops were meant to build both teachers' computer skills and their interest in the program. Teachers could choose what to study, and instruction focused on skills and resources that could be immediately applied in the classroom.

At the time, many teachers were interested in learning PowerPoint. Students were hired as tutors and paired with teachers, shadowing them and helping them complete projects. The only thing these student tutors were told, says Levin, was "don't touch the keyboard or the mouse, just be the guide." These weeklong workshops proved to be very successful. They encouraged technology integration efforts in subsequent school years and helped prepare teachers to take on the challenges that the 1-to-1 laptop program presented when it was first rolled out.

While teachers' instructional methods overall may not have changed drastically since the laptop program began, Levin sees indisputable evidence that teaching practices are evolving due to the many different things made possible when students and teachers have 24/7 access to a laptop computer. Urban has always encouraged a student-centered, project-based learning environment, and laptops have enabled teachers to take that approach to the next level. The digital storytelling project Telling Their Stories is a perfect example of this: without laptops and ubiquitous access to the Internet and video editing software, this project would not have been nearly so successful.

GETTING ADMINISTRATORS AND PARENTS ON BOARD

Salkind was on board with the concept of 1-to-1 laptops from the beginning, as evidenced by his hiring of Levin to help implement and evangelize the program. Salkind's support was crucial, Levin says, and because of it, convincing other administrators of the merits of the program wasn't a problem. Convincing the Board of Trustees proved to be a little more difficult, however. Salkind and Levin moved slowly and carefully with the board, since there were few laptop programs in the Bay Area to point to for success stories and comparisons.

Initially, figuring out how to pay for the laptop program was also a big challenge. Today, student laptops are purchased with a parent-user fee that equals the 3-year leased value of the computer. Parents are given the necessary information in print, and there's no opt-out option. Many other schools couldn't do this, Levin admits, but it works at Urban because Urban parents have such a high degree of trust in the Head of School and the Board of Trustees. Consequently, getting the parents on board really was a matter of getting the Board of Trustees firmly on board first.

To increase the board's awareness of the potential of laptops in education, a technology task force was formed, comprising several board members as well as Salkind and Levin. Urban sent this team to the Dalton School in New York City and to Cincinnati Country Day School in Ohio to view their programs. The team then developed a laptop implementation plan for The Urban School and brought this proposal to the rest of the board.

A key selling point was the task force's assertion that a laptop program wouldn't cost the school a significant amount of money. This was important because a survey of Urban families showed that 78% to 80% of them already had a computer, or were planning to buy one. A school-mandated but parent-funded laptop program, then, would simply redirect funds that were being spent anyway so that everyone could benefit. In the end, there was very little disagreement about what was anticipated to be the biggest problem: cost was really a nonissue. The laptop proposal received unanimous board approval.

PROGRAM SUCCESSES

Levin says that increased collaboration and sharing of information is "the No. 1 positive change universally felt by everyone" involved in the laptop program. Urban uses First Class, an e-mail program installed at many schools. According to Levin this communication tool is "the cornerstone of what we do." Teachers appreciate how easy it now is to share information with other teachers, students, and parents, and how that can lead to better integration and organization of curriculum across all content areas.

Another big success of the program has been the dramatic increase in the use of computer technology by everyone at the school. This was both an overt and covert priority, says Levin: "We didn't talk much about it...[but] it was one of my objectives from the start. Knowing technology gives kids an enormous advantage." While kids at The Urban School don't consider themselves to be particularly tech-savvy because they don't take technology classes, their proficiency with computers is actually quite high, Levin says. Simply by using laptops to do all their schoolwork, they quickly become comfortable with the hardware and software, to the point students are increasingly doing their own tech support and helping each other fix problems.

HOW LAPTOPS ARE USED AT URBAN

Levin says that "communication, organization, information and production" have been enhanced by laptops at The Urban School (personal communication, November 23, 2004). He points to the example of Urban science department chair Algis Sodonis. Sodonis posts online solutions to difficult problems and maintains an archive of Help files and exemplary student work.

In keeping with Urban's constructivist philosophy, collaborative work and project-based learning are major elements of the curriculum, requiring students to plan and organize their workloads independently. Levin says that surveys of Urban students confirm that enhancing their ability to stay organized and keep track of projects is seen as a primary benefit of having laptops 24/7: "When asked about the best school-related use of their laptop, 63% of student narrative responses dealt with organization" (ibid.). Laptops give Urban students access to specialized resources: students in the constitutional law class use the Web resource FindLaw (www.findlaw.com) to research laws in ways that were previously possible only by visiting a law library. Teachers use their laptops to hold online conferences with writing groups to encourage student collaboration on projects.

Levin concludes that Urban's laptop program "is smoothly making the transition from its earlier experimental phase to one where use is becoming more truly seamless, ubiquitous and normal. The reported advantages are also helping to support a truly dynamic curriculum filled with a sense of new possibilities" (ibid.).

Whitfield School, St. Louis

Whitfield School is an independent, non-parochial school in St. Louis, Missouri, that enrolls 475 boys and girls in Grades 6–12. Director of Technology Alex Inman, who previously developed a 1-to-1 initiative at a school in Wisconsin, is drawing on that experience to plan and implement Whitfield's new laptop program. Inman's plan is to roll out the 1-to-1 laptop program for all Whitfield School students over the course of 4 years.

The program was launched in the 2004–2005 school year, when laptops were provided to all Whitfield teachers and a limited number of students. During this first year, there were two carts of laptops that could be rolled from class to class, and three pilot classrooms.

Initial funding was obtained through a self-funded grant competition called UTSUT (Uber-Teachers Seeking Ubiquity with Technology). Eight or nine Whitfield teachers applied. They agreed to be the program's "indentured servants" for at least 3 years, working with the laptops in their own classrooms the first year and then teaching others how to use them effectively over the next 2. It was tough to determine the grant recipients, says Inman, because many qualified teachers applied: "We picked people who were good at professional development."

Whitfield took this "gradual rollout" approach both to create a manageable experience set within the school and for financial reasons. Gradual rollout enables teachers and administrators to better manage the changes in learning environment and teaching practice that ubiquitous computing entails. It also creates a committed cadre of experts who can help colleagues figure out how to integrate laptops into their classrooms with as little disruption as possible. Whitfield's gradual approach has also allowed it to absorb the cost of the program in more digestible and sustainable chunks.

Rather than funding laptops as a one-time capital expense, Whitfield has chosen a "phased lease" approach that helps to create a defined timeframe for the laptops and permits more predictable annual budget planning. By implementing the program gradually, the school's been able to fund not only the initial cost of the laptops themselves but also the operational and network costs associated with their introduction. Inman says a similar approach will be used to build in upgrades to the hardware as the program continues to grow in the years ahead: the newest laptop models will go to faculty and seniors, the year-old models will go to 10th- and 11th-graders, the 2-year-old models will go to 8th- and 9th-graders, and so forth. This way, as students become older and more sophisticated users, they'll get newer and more powerful computers to use.

Together, this phased lease approach and the gradual rollout has allowed Whitfield to roll the cost of the laptop program into each student's tuition fees. Since tuition is the main source of funding for instructional programs at Whitfield, administrators were concerned that they not raise tuition too precipitously to fund the laptop program. By going with the gradual rollout and the 4-year leasing arrangement, Inman says, the school was able to limit the technology-related tuition hike to about $150 per year per student.

GETTING THE PROGRAM STARTED

Whitfield School follows a process-oriented instructional philosophy, focusing more time and energy on the overall learning process than on any particular academic discipline's content. Grade-level teams meet once a week so that teachers can coordinate curricula and collaboratively implement cross-curricular projects.

When Inman first came to visit the school at the invitation of Whitfield President Mark Anderson, he was immediately inspired by this student-centered approach. He remembers his first impression of the school (personal communication, December 15, 2004):

> [President Anderson] gave me three hours and said, "Go where you want and wander around." In that time, I saw only one teacher standing at a board. Every other class had students working in groups. This school really espoused a student-centered model of teaching. I was sold!

Inman responded so readily to Whitfield's process-oriented instruction because he believes that while teaching content is fine, a lot of that content eventually becomes obsolete. What's more important, he thinks, is to teach students how to "garner, gather and synthesize information so that students are prepared to learn and create new knowledge in the future." Whitfield's instructional approach is perfect for making that happen on a daily basis: "All of the tools and approaches I have brought in here have found a home almost immediately."

When Inman came on board at Whitfield, school president Anderson accompanied him on a tour of six laptop-using schools in the area (**P** for planning). In their subsequent report to Whitfield's Board of Trustees, they indicated that much of what they'd seen in these programs was disappointing. The technology was simply being used to automate the same teacher-centered modes of instruction that had been in place before. Many of these schools had pointed excitedly to their use of electronic SmartBoards, some funded by the Missouri eMints program. However, Inman and Anderson felt the SmartBoards were only facilitating and automating the "sage on the stage" teaching methods that Whitfield wanted to avoid. Inman says (ibid.):

> Though we saw some great things, we saw too many teachers making the technology fit an existing model of teaching rather than letting the technology be a more transparent tool... SmartBoards and projectors are great tools, but if they only further entrench the teacher's power in the front of the room rather than help students facilitate their own learning, the school is not getting the full educational value for their investment in laptops.

Inman and Salkind worked on creating a laptop program that would reflect Whitfield's process-oriented philosophy and make learning a student-centered activity. Seeing how other schools in the area were using technology helped Whitfield design their own program.

IMPLEMENTING THE PROGRAM

Whitfield is in the second year of its 4-year gradual rollout. Much remains to be done before administrators and teachers will be able to confidently evaluate the laptop program's overall effects on Whitfield's learning environment. Major pedagogical changes of all types typically take 3 to 5 years to take effect, so Inman believes Whitfield's laptop initiative is on the right timetable.

Having led a similar program at University Lake School, Inman has the advantage of experience. He recalls one student there (a relative of one of the school's founders) who, when laptops were first handed out during his sophomore year, called them "$1,600 paperweights" that would quickly become "$1,600 music storage systems." Two years later, Inman taught him in one of his senior classes and noticed that the laptop never left his side. Inman asked the student what he thought of his paperweight now. He responded that he could no longer imagine living without it: his research and writing was much improved, and he was so much more organized than before. He'd devised a number of ways to use the laptop to help him with his studies. Rather than using index cards to organize the 50 resources needed for a history project, for example, he'd developed an Access database with hyperlinks. His database model was so useful, the history teacher had been using it on other projects ever since. "The kid did it," Inman remembers. "He understood the goal and context, understood the tool, and brought it to the next level" (ibid.).

Similar things are already happening at Whitfield School. In 11th-grade English classes, for example, students are required to identify a truth that's important to them or their generation and design a book cover that depicts both the truth and their perspective on it. The project is intended to help students learn to communicate in an increasingly visual world. After students have designed their covers, the covers are displayed and a jury of peers tries to intuit the truth depicted as well as the designer's perspective on that truth.

Before Whitfield 11th-graders had laptops, most students created their book covers by cutting out images from magazines and making a collage. When laptops became available, however, students asked for and received permission to use digital tools for the project. They looked for images on the Internet, took their own digital photos or scanned and manipulated existing images, and assembled their covers using Adobe Photoshop.

The English teacher in charge reports that students seemed considerably more involved in the project when using digital tools, and their designs communicated their intended message to the student juries 90% of the time. When covers were designed using the old magazine cutout method, student juries were typically able to identify the truth depicted only 50% of the time. Inman says (personal communication, December 10, 2004) this is precisely the kind of anecdotal evidence that is most persuasive to him.

> This project was done during the pilot phase of a laptop rollout plan. We believe deeply in a notion of a community of learners in which teachers have just as much to learn from the students as the students do from the teachers. I believe this understanding is critical for the success of a laptop program... Many of our teachers speak "technology" only as a second language whereas many students speak "technology" as a fluid part of their day-to-day lives. This teacher created an environment in which students felt comfortable challenging the design of the assignment, and the teacher was comfortable being challenged. What resulted was a more appropriate and more challenging lesson.

1-to-1 access to laptops gave these Whitfield students the ability to communicate more precisely using digital images and tools. By giving them a chance to select, manipulate, and own their own digital designs, the entire project had more meaning for them. This is an exemplar of what can happen when teachers and administrators are open to process-oriented curricular design facilitated by laptops.

The laptop rollout has not been without its problems and challenges, of course. Inman mentions two in particular: hardware maintenance and teacher training. He cautions schools considering a laptop program to plan carefully for the challenges of keeping hundreds of laptops up and running while simultaneously maintaining the viability and security of the school network: "This is hard but has to be done" (ibid.).

With regard to training teachers to use laptops more effectively in the classroom, Inman says what's most important is to teach them to enhance their existing curriculum by using the standard features of their computers creatively rather than relying on canned digital material. "[Laptops] can be a sweet catalyst to get teachers to think about curriculum, and think differently," says Inman, leading to more dynamic, process-oriented teaching practices (ibid.).

HOW LAPTOPS ARE USED AT WHITFIELD

During the 2005–2006 school year, all 11th- and 12th- graders at Whitfield were given laptops for the first time. Inman was immediately impressed with how well they were integrated into the classroom. The 12th-grade history class at Whitfield quickly became paperless. Laptops enabled students to work on the NAIS Challenge 20/20 project—a global schools initiative created by the National Association of Independent Schools—and interact with students at a school in Germany by means of an online Web portal.

"Laptops [are] used nearly daily for research, writing, electronic communication, and presentations," Inman says. Individual projects include the use of Photoshop in 11th-grade history classes to create stamp designs that "represent a decade within the context of a single event or person" (ibid.). Twelfth-grade math classes use laptops to graph solutions and take online quizzes. In both 11th- and 12th-grade science, students work in online virtual labs and use probes that can be attached to the laptops to measure force and temperature. Inman says (personal communication, December 28, 2005):

> In foreign language classes, the free audio-editing program Audacity is used to record and play back conversations so that students can hear and improve their pronunciation. Students are asked to do impromptu research on a regular basis: "When a conversation or discussion in class yields an interesting question, the teacher takes advantage of that teachable moment to assign students to do a little instant online research and find different perspectives or answers to that question."

The Denver School of Science and Technology

While the other schools profiled in this chapter had their own institutional history of earlier school reforms and improvements to draw on when they implemented their laptop programs, this was not the case for The Denver School of Science and Technology (DSST). Whereas both The Urban School and Whitfield School carefully considered how to adapt their existing structures to accommodate a laptop program that would support and further their school mission, DSST gave all of its teachers and students laptops from the moment it first opened its doors in 2004. Founded and funded by grants from the Bill and Melinda Gates Foundation and other benefactors, it's the first public school in Colorado to provide laptops to all students.

On the school Web site (www.scienceandtech.org/), the founding of the school is described as the result of a conversation between Bill Gates and Colorado governor Bill Owens about educating students more thoroughly in math and science.

Mark Inglis, director of technology at DSST, describes the school's approach to technology integration in this way (personal communication, July 28, 2005):

> We seek to enable and support transformative uses of technology... If technology is simply used to do things that students could do in other ways—if it is used only to enhance rather than transform what they are learning—then it is not worthwhile.

DSST provides laptops to all of its students to engage them and motivate them to experience learning in ways that would be impossible without laptops. These include direct communication with researchers in the field, collaboration using wikis and blogs and other tools, computer-enhanced student-to-student, teacher-to-student, and school-to-parent interactions, and so forth.

When asked about the challenges of launching the DSST laptop program, Inglis emphasized the importance of transparency. Making technology transparent for all users and getting everything to work from day one is difficult but doable with good planning, he says. Funding and staffing are crucial issues: Inglis himself runs the school network and provides tech support, and a .5 FTE staff member is dedicated to working with faculty and students on technology integration. He says administrators must carefully consider the workload of teachers who must learn how to teach effectively with technology: "Nearly all teachers are overworked to begin with, and when they have to learn some new technology and how to teach with it, it takes time on their part. Finding the energy and resources for teachers is significant work" (ibid.).

Laptop cases were another start-up challenge. Initially, the school provided laptop cases for every student. However, finding cost-effective cases that would stand up to the rigors of student use proved difficult. Consequently, they now require students to either buy a backpack built especially for the laptop or purchase a used case from the school. Most choose the former. Inglis has also looked into the always-on cases available from such vendors as InfoCase and now believes they're the better option. In the future, he plans to offer this option to families.

No retrofitting was needed for wireless access since the brand new school building was outfitted with numerous wireless access points. Lockers weren't part of the original design, but they've since been added. "We originally had laptop 'pigeonholes' throughout the building that could be secured with a cable," Inglis says, "but since we found that students were having a hard time remembering their AC adapters, we thought the same might happen with the cables and keys" (ibid.). Consequently, laptop-friendly lockers have been installed for those rare times when the laptops are out of students' hands.

Despite DSST's short history, the school has already succeeded in ways that differentiate it from other, more traditional schools. "If I were to pick one [success]," Inglis says, "it would be in communication. Between all parties. Students, staff, teacher to student… everyone communicates far more and far better because everyone is connected wirelessly all the time" (ibid.). Inglis echoes other educators at laptop-using schools by saying that students at DSST seem far more engaged when using technology, and attendance problems have been virtually nonexistent (see http://scienceandtech.org/results.html for school academic results).

GETTING TEACHERS ONBOARD

Teachers knew what they were getting into when they applied for jobs at DSST: "Everyone knew students would have laptops and teachers would be expected to use them," Inglis says (ibid.). Still, there were some initial challenges getting these teachers to integrate the technology into their normal teaching practices. This figured into the school's decision to go with tablet PCs rather than laptops in the second year of the program. Tablets were a natural for math, but not every teacher was immediately comfortable with them.

As the school's first year came to a close and teachers received their performance reviews, specific issues were addressed and professional development needs were identified. Teachers who felt confident in their technology skills were dispatched to help those colleagues who felt less comfortable. "It's impossible to do as much [teacher professional development] as I'd like," Inglis says. "We do some [workshops] every year before school starts, and we would like to do more ongoing sessions on an intentional, not reactionary, basis" (ibid.).

"I think you can't overdo professional development, and the more exhaustive workshops you do, the better off you'll be," Inglis says (ibid.). He recommends that school or district administrators who want to improve their professional development program in support of laptop integration should look for ideas from colleagues who have "been there, done that." Inglis himself contacted the Cincinnati Country Day School and the Henrico County School District in Virginia, and both were very helpful in the planning process at DSST. Good planning and flexibility, along with establishing a solid infrastructure from the beginning, are all key components for program success. When it comes to student technology training, on the other hand, he recommends (ibid.) that it always be contextualized as part of a project or curricular activities.

> We don't have any formal, ongoing student training. Our philosophy is that in order for this [technology] to be transformative, the training needs to be in the context of learning. As [students] are writing research papers, or working in Geometer's Sketchpad, they are learning the technology. We have instituted a mandatory 'seminar' class that teaches introductory skills and a few pieces of software (e.g., Dreamweaver) required for more independent projects such as our Digital Portfolio.

CO-OPTING TECH-SAVVY STUDENTS

DSST has found that a good way to empower students and encourage their active involvement in school is to use them as technical support specialists. "Our tech support crew is about 20 or 25 students," says Inglis. Students work to keep the laptops' software and operating system up-to-date and operational. DSST typically re-clones its computers during the school year to ensure they have the latest updates and are running optimally: "First we tell students to make sure they have all of their files backed up. Then we have the student tech support crew gather and clone all of the computers." Using students for tech support increases productivity and reduces the down-time when laptops are out of student hands. "Last year, we took 2½ days to re-clone all the laptops. This year, we did it in a day and a half. We expect it to take no more than a day next year" (ibid.).

Membership in the tech support crew is open to any DSST student but requires recommendations from an advisor, a teacher, a non-tech crew student, and a sponsoring member of the current tech crew. An extensive training and observation process takes place, after which students become full-fledged members and are allowed to use the local admin password to work on all laptops. Two-thirds of the tech crew are 10th-graders and the rest are 9th-graders. Their contribution is essential to keeping laptops up and running.

One of the great benefits of this program is that it tends to co-opt the most tech-savvy (and potentially most trouble-making) students and encourages them to use their skills to good purpose. With the tech crew's emphasis on integrity and responsibility, combined with a reasonable dose of power, this program provides an incentive for fledgling hackers to work toward a positive goal.

HOW LAPTOPS ARE USED AT DSST

Students at DSST take their laptops with them everywhere they go: "They're used almost every moment of the day, except for gym class," says Inglis (ibid.). While some of this constant usage undoubtedly involves Web games and social communication, a lot of homework's being done. In fact, the vast majority of assignments at DSST are delivered via computer. Some teachers notify students of assignments by creating Outlook calendar appointments and sending them to a distribution group. This puts the assignment and all its details directly onto the students' calendars and takes advantage of Outlook's automatic reminder feature. In this way, assignments can be accessed by students anytime and anywhere they have an Internet connection. Students can see the assignments, plan their work, and keep track of their progress, all in one location.

At school, the file server provides a drop box and class resource folder for teachers and students to share work back and forth. Students can access their own individual network folders, but no one else's. Teachers can retrieve homework assignments from the class drop box and return them directly to individual students' folders.

Last year, DSST introduced Tablet PCs to all their sophomores. According to Inglis, "Virtually all of our 10th-grade teachers now use tablets on a daily basis, because it allows students to take notes in their own handwriting" (ibid.). Tablet PCs have built-in microphones that teachers have used to do student interviews, while language teachers have used the same capabilities to record language lessons and speaking practice. Presentation software is commonly used by both teachers and students.

DSST students are also required to create and post materials and work samples in a digital portfolio, a series of Web pages used for goal-setting and assessment. According to the DSST Web site, "The Digital Portfolio (DP) will be a core academic assessment tool accessible to the entire school community...[and] will include a student's resume and a statement about his/her learning goals and achievements. Samples of a student's best work will be showcased and archived through the digital portfolios."

Other interesting software tools being used at DSST include SynchronEyes, a program designed for student computer management and control, and Microsoft OneNote, a collaborative document creation program that allows teachers and students to work together on brainstorming sessions, collective composition, and peer editing for written assignments. Recently, DSST teachers have begun to use Exam View, a network-based testing program that allows the creation of classroom tests that can be tied, question-by-question, to Colorado's state content area standards.

Chapter 3
DISTRICT-WIDE AND STATEWIDE PROGRAMS

Introduction

IT'S ONE THING to deploy a few hundred laptops in a single school building. It's something else again when laptop numbers run to five figures and the deployment is across an entire school district or state. The planning, logistics, politics, and infrastructure issues—not to mention the media attention likely to follow—can be quite daunting. Fortunately, for those of us watching and learning, a number of school districts across the country as well as a few states have taken a leap of faith and inaugurated large-scale laptop programs.

This chapter profiles laptop programs instituted by Henrico County, Virginia; Maine; and Michigan. All three programs were kind enough to allow me to interview key planners and administrators. I've distilled their firsthand experiences in the descriptions that follow. Each of these programs has also received considerable media scrutiny, some of which is referenced here.

Figure 3.1
Teaching 1-to-1 becomes a reality when the student has a laptop computer.

Henrico County, Virginia

Lloyd Brown, director of technology at Henrico County School District in Virgina, spoke to me about the district's laptop program. One of the first large-scale laptop initiatives in the United States, Henrico is currently in the fifth year of its district-wide program. Henrico found itself growing rapidly at the end of the '90s and struggling to keep up with changes in education technology, wondering how best to outfit its existing and new classrooms. The district's commitment (**C**) to graduating students with solid, transferable computer skills was strong, but they had an older school district with older buildings and not enough computer labs. The usual solutions seemed inadequate to the district's needs.

Fortunately, Henrico County leaders were ready and willing to consider all options and were unafraid to take some risks. Their commitment to providing students with the best technology tools possible encouraged them to take an aggressive approach to addressing the district's technology needs.

The district didn't want to start converting classrooms into computer labs and displacing students because most schools simply didn't have enough space or electrical capacity for this kind of expansion. Nor, with enrollment rising, did the district have the capital resources necessary to replace the old schools with expensive high-tech ones. District administrators looked briefly at a plan to install six or so computers per classroom, but the same issue—lack of space and electrical capacity—made this plan untenable.

Consequently, Henrico formed a committee of district and site administrators to look at other ways to provide technology to their students (**P** for planning). The conversation soon moved to laptops, since these machines were getting smaller and more durable. Once they began considering different ways they could deploy laptops throughout the district, a consensus emerged in favor of a 1-to-1 initiative.

Brown took part in this planning right from the beginning, undertaking a "total cost of ownership" study to consider laptops for every student in the district. It quickly became apparent to him that buying hardware and putting it in place for 6 or 7 years wouldn't further the district's overall goal of giving students the opportunity to use and learn the newest technologies. Eventually, the antiquated hardware would become unusable, and the software that ran on it would no longer be transferable to the business world. Brown decided that leasing laptops made the most sense for the district, since that meant the hardware would be renewed every 4 years.

Henrico aggressively negotiated the leasing arrangement to lower costs enough to provide 18,000 laptops the first year of the program (2000–2001). Today, that number's up to 29,000, enough laptops to outfit every teacher in the district as well as all middle and high school students.

Cautionary Tale

Dealing with Inappropriate Downloads

One of the things we can learn from Henrico is flexibility. Things you don't expect to happen will happen. It's how you respond that counts. During the first year of the Henrico laptop program, some students were found downloading music and pornography to their laptops. This caused a few naysayers to jump on the ever popular "we told you so" bandwagon. Henrico responded by recalling the computers, reformatting them, upping their memory and security, and closing network loopholes. Inappropriate downloads haven't been a major problem since.

Knowing that getting buy-in from teachers (**E** for educators) was key, Henrico invested a lot of time and professional development dollars getting faculty comfortable and ready for the new program. Teachers were shown how the new laptops could be used to build a stronger school-to-home bridge and increase communication and accountability with parents and students. Increased teacher productivity was also addressed by implementing an electronic grading system. The goal of these professional development efforts, Brown says, was to encourage teachers to believe that "technology should work for me, not the other way around."

These outreach efforts quickly paid off, as teachers warmed to the benefits of 1-to-1 computing. But starting up such a program—one that had to be implemented at several different sites simultaneously—was not without its challenges. Brown initially felt it would take 5 years to get the program fully off the ground given the huge pedagogical and cultural changes that needed to take place across the district.

However, Henrico's School Board remained firm in its support and gave the district Technology Department the time it needed to work out all of the initial bugs. After piloting the program in 2000–2001, Brown and his team spent the summer planning (**P**) how to provide wireless networking for every laptop in every building. They carefully calculated bandwidth needs so that everyone would be able to connect to the Internet from their laptops. By the third year of the program, most teachers were comfortable with it, and more professional development training was scheduled to help teachers integrate computers into their classrooms.

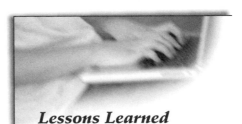

Lessons Learned

Henrico's Kid-Friendly Laptop Support Page

Henrico has put together a very kid-friendly area of their Web site. It provides useful information about using and caring for a laptop computer. With its colorful locker room entrance, playful fonts, and concise and simple information, this site is well worth your look. They even have an Apple-to-Dell comparison to help their high school students make the transition to new laptops. Go to http://staffdev.henrico.k12.va.us/students/index.html.

HOW LAPTOPS ARE USED IN HENRICO COUNTY SCHOOLS

With nearly 30,000 laptops in the program today, Henrico has the purchasing power to negotiate good prices for the software and peripherals they include with their laptops. Tech planners have taken advantage of this to provide teachers and students with a wide variety of learning programs and productivity software. Among the most popular programs used by Henrico teachers are the following:

▶ Beyond Books offers online curriculum that extends in-class exercises with Web links, worksheets, organizers, and self-assessing features.

▶ Explore Learning offers interactive math and science simulations called Gizmos.

▶ Larson's Pre-Algebra helps math teachers customize their curriculum and testing.

▶ Apex Learning provides accelerated activities and assessment tools optimized for advanced placement students.

▶ Quia offers Web-based tools for creating interactive games, flashcards, word searches, and other reinforcement applications.

Another popular application available to students and teachers in the district is Virtual Share, a file-sharing program that allows teachers to upload assignments and documents to the school's server. It also allows students to send homework from home or school to the teacher's drop box (Henrico County Public Schools Web site, www.henrico.k12.va.us/laptopinitiative/, downloaded January 1, 2006).

From the beginning, one of the primary goals of Henrico County's laptop program has been to encourage innovative teaching:

> We wanted...fewer lectures and more engaged, active learning using dynamic, current content... Today, in many of our classrooms, there is a new sense of discovery and the feel of a research laboratory. Every student has access to a universe of online libraries. A class exploring Italian Renaissance artists, for example, reaches a depth and breadth of study well beyond what they would have been exposed to previously. (eSchool news, 2006)

Along with these new instructional methodologies have come improvements in test scores:

> After 2 years of a laptop initiative in Henrico County, high school score results increased on all 11 of the Virginia Standards of Learning tests. In 2000, only 60% of Henrico's regular schools were accredited according to Virginia Standards of Learning criteria. By 2003, 100% of Henrico's regular schools were accredited. This includes 40 elementary schools, 11 middle schools, and 9 high schools. (Barrios, 2004, p. 22)

Another important lesson to be learned from Henrico's experience is the role laptops can play in making the home-to-school transition seamless and fluid. Since Henrico subsidizes low-cost Internet access for students and teachers who don't have access in their homes (www.henrico.k12.va.us/laptopinitiative/, downloaded January 1, 2006), the transfer of homework, assignments, evaluations, and communications with teachers becomes ubiquitous and easy. Laptops have made it easier for educators to determine if students are learning and for students to demonstrate that they've learned.

Brown allows that there's always more to be done. Public school education has changed drastically in the 25 years he's worked as an educator, and instructional approaches and learning resources continue to evolve and improve. He believes, however, that Henrico's laptop program has placed the district in a better position to respond to those changes quickly and effectively. The program has given its teachers and students access to the tools they'll need to succeed in the 21st century.

As far as sustainability is concerned, Brown says Henrico is committed to maintaining the current size of the program for at least 4 more years. They recently signed a 4-year lease agreement with Dell after severing a similar lease with Apple.

Henrico is also committed to studying the effects of 1-to-1 computing on student achievement and behavior. Several researchers are planning studies. Brown cautions, however, that it will be difficult to tie the results of these studies directly to scores on state-mandated standardized tests, both because of the way those tests are administered and because what the tests are measuring are not necessarily influenced by technology.

Cautionary Tale

Repairs, Recycling, and Media Attention

In August 2005, Henrico decided to switch from the Apple laptops they began their program with to Dell. The district decided to sell their used iBooks for $50 each. After first offering them to district staff, they advertised the laptops to county residents, holding the sale at a local racetrack. If you're still unsure of the popularity and demand for laptops, just go to the following Web site and read the *Washington Post* article regarding the melee that followed: www.washingtonpost.com/wp-dyn/content/article/2005/08/16/AR2005081600738.html.

The State of Maine

The story of Maine's statewide laptop program is fascinating. In December 1999, faced with something every state governor wants—a budgetary surplus—then-Governor Angus King realized there was enough money available to really make a difference in education in his state. He began to cast around for ideas (Kim, 2002).

Dr. Seymour Papert, a Maine resident and researcher at MIT, where he co-developed the educational programming language Logo and published numerous influential books on computers, learning, and artificial intelligence, was called in to meet with the governor. The governor asked Dr. Papert what he thought would happen if the state government equipped every school in Maine with enough computers to lower the student-to-computer ratio to 3-to-1 or even 2-to-1. To the governor's surprise, the MIT scientist said, in effect, nothing much: "It only turns magic when it's 1-to-1" (Apple Learning Exchange). To his great credit as a leader, King took this advice and ran with it. In March 2000 he announced his plan to provide every seventh-grader in Maine with a laptop computer.

Dr. Mike Muir, director of the Maine Center for Meaningful Engaged Learning (www. mcmel.org), spoke to me at length about the founding of this program and the challenges he and others faced in turning this lunchtime conversation into a reality. He and other representatives of the University of Maine system were brought in in August 2001 to help with the planning stages (**P**) of this ambitious program. A committee was formed called the Design Team for Curriculum and Professional Development, and Bette Manchester, an award-winning principal and Distinguished Educator in Maine, was appointed its leader. I had the pleasure of interviewing Manchester at a recent 1-to-1 symposium, and her comments also inform this profile of Maine's laptop program.

The Maine Learning Technology Initiative (MLTI) was formally established in the winter of 2002, with the stated goal of providing "the tools and training necessary to ensure that Maine's students become the most technologically savvy students in the world" (www. state.me.us/mlte/). The Design Team worked in the summer of 2001 to bring together teachers, administrators, and university professors to set goals and establish the ground-work for the MLTI. According to Dr. Muir, a formal Request for Proposal (RFP) process was in place by the end of that summer, and a hardware vendor (Apple Computer) was selected by the committee in the winter of 2001–2002 (personal communication, August 4, 2005).

Around the same time, Dr. Muir was given a half-release from his university teaching load to direct a federal PT^3 technology grant. While it was still not clear what the state was planning to do with the laptops, he saw obvious and useful connections between this state laptop initiative and his PT^3 grant, so he looked for ways to get involved in the administrative end of the project.

Manchester made it clear from the outset that MLTI needed to reach out to teachers directly and involve them (**E** for Educators). She believes there's too often a disconnect between the promises made by education technology visionaries and the actual imple-mentation of technology in schools. That disconnect, she says, comes from a lack of empowered, knowledgeable teachers and technology leaders in individual school districts.

The vision and driving force behind the Maine laptop program may have come initially from the governor's office, but Manchester knew that a purely political mandate would not be enough to make this program successful. She sought for ways to empower teachers and technology leaders to take an active role in the planning and implementation process. Consequently, teacher leaders, principals, and technology coordinators from every district and middle school in the state were identified, and an e-mail database was created to facilitate communication.

According to Manchester (personal communication, November 23, 2005), this collaborative method of planning has been instrumental in the program's success:

> This is about shared leadership and shared ownership...[We wanted to] pay attention to the transition, pay attention to the changes that stakeholders were going through, their fear factors, [so as to] develop and sustain a sense of a learning community.

In taking this approach, the leaders of the MLTI were intentionally modeling what they wanted to happen in 1-to-1 laptop classrooms. They've sustained this learning community by continuing to convene regular face-to-face meetings with stakeholders. Manchester says (ibid.):

> Our meetings with principals, technology personnel, and teacher leaders are held within each of the nine superintendent regions in Maine. Thirty building leadership groups meet within each region. During the first 2 years of the project, we met 3 or 4 times a year along with a 2½ day retreat for the teacher leaders and 2-day workshops for the leadership team regarding the change process, embedding technology in the curriculum, and data driven decision making. We continue to meet twice a year during the school year in each region of the state, convening 30 schools at a time in the fall and spring. We also hold workshops each year at the principals' conference.

Daylong staff development meetings are held with teachers in each of the nine regions twice a year, offering training in literacy, math, science, information literacy, and project-based learning. Altogether, there were 7 full days of professional development available to all content area teachers in every region during the 2005–2006 school year. This was in addition to summer institutes and workshops held throughout the state during the summer months. In previous years, there were as many as 10 days of professional development. Manchester adds (personal communication, January 2, 2006), "We also go and work with teachers at school sites, upon request. Twice a year, workshops are held for those who are the technology integrators in the schools. Apple and MLTI do workshops for all tech directors as well."

While Maine wasn't the first educational body to provide laptops to students and teachers, it was the first state to do so on a massive scale. More than 37,000 laptops were deployed in 239 middle schools (Muir, Manchester, & Moulton, 2005, p. 1). Initially, keeping everyone informed of the program's progress was a major challenge, Dr. Muir recalls (personal communication, August 4, 2005):

> By February of 2002, teacher leaders, technology staff, and principals were all coming to us saying "Why didn't we get this information?" The fact is, we were giving them information, as soon as we got it ourselves. They just thought we already had [more information], when we didn't.

In response to this overwhelming demand for more information, Muir formed a team to make a half-hour documentary on the laptop initiative that was distributed to schools to inform teachers and principals and ease concerns. Funding for this documentary was provided through Muir's PT[3] grant.

When asked what she might do differently if given the chance to start the program over, Manchester says she would make sure "that the same people working on the laptop project have the funds to prepare building principals and superintendents." She mentions a particular grant from the Bill and Melinda Gates Foundation that was awarded in

November 2000 to Maine's Department of Education to improve administrators' use of technology (Maine.gov Web site www.state.me.us/newsletter/backissues/nov2000/leading_to_change.htm, downloaded January 2, 2006). She wishes now that she could have used that money to prepare principals and superintendents for the laptop initiative.

Instead of teaching technical skills, she says (personal communication, November 23, 2005), this training should have tackled leadership issues:

> Working on leadership with principals and superintendents needs to be cyclical and systematic...People in leadership roles cycle in and out of Maine. Perhaps they are new to their position; others are new to technology. There should be a way to formalize and make systemic the teaching of technology leadership, especially [for a program that] is this important.

Dr. Muir says that everyone involved in the early stages of the MLTI knew they needed to start collecting data immediately on how the use of laptops was affecting teaching and learning. The sheer size and complexity of the project, however, delayed this evaluation. The Maine Education Policy Research Institute (MEPRI) was charged with evaluating how students' learning styles were responding to the ubiquitous presence of laptops. Additional research was conducted by the Mitchell Institute, the Maine Learning with Laptop Studies (Mike Muir, Gerald Knezek, and Rhonda Christensen), and Gail Gartwaite.

The MEPRI studies constitute an excellent and comprehensive body of research. Anyone considering a laptop program would do well to spend some time with these reports (www.usm.maine.edu/cepare/mlti.htm). These studies show that students with laptops are more engaged in their learning and have a greater ability to explore, analyze, and communicate, while teachers in laptop classrooms are varying their lessons and using newer resources (Muir, Manchester, & Moulton, 2005, Summer).

PROGRAM GOALS, OFFICIAL AND OTHERWISE

The original goal of the MLTI was, in part, to improve the economy of Maine. Governor King realized that Maine wouldn't remain economically competitive for long if the state didn't try something new and ambitious with its educational programs. While this economic goal remains at the heart of MLTI, the program, from the start, had other, less official, goals.

The Design Team's unofficial goals included improved learning and teaching in Maine middle schools. To realize this goal, the team believed it was important for the program to focus on instruction and professional development rather than on hardware and software. This caused some disagreement along the way. Dr. Muir recalls (personal communication, August 4, 2005):

> Although some wanted straight technology training, the Design Team recommended doing training in the context of teaching with technology. Instead of doing workshops on spreadsheets, for example, we wanted to teach teachers to analyze data *using* spreadsheets.

While Dr. Muir believes the program's professional development goals have largely been realized, he cautions that it's difficult to draw connections between this professional development focus and student achievement under the MLTI. While there's a lot of anecdotal evidence that teachers are teaching differently with laptops, and that Maine middle school students are now more engaged in their learning and have better attendance and fewer behavioral referrals, Dr. Muir admits that these outcomes could simply be evidence of a Hawthorne effect.

Dr. Muir believes the state has been "hit hard by NCLB" and its ideas about highly qualified teachers and local assessments. Still, professional development must be an ongoing effort: "Resistant or cautious teachers making professional advancements need to be nurtured and supported" (ibid.).

While most stories collected by evaluators of the MLTI have been success stories, stories about teachers having a hard time and not integrating laptops into their teaching have also been told. Manchester emphasizes the importance of establishing and sustaining a professional development network for teachers and administrators involved in the 1-to-1 program: "Your network has to be both face-to-face and virtual. There has to be a place to put resources, including Web presences—a place for teachers to collaborate and share material." In Maine, that place is www.mainelearns.org.

HIGH SCHOOLS—THE NEXT STEP

While the initial plan was to provide laptops to all seventh- and eighth-graders as they moved through the system, Maine officials began to strategize how best to extend the program into high schools as well. Thirty-nine high schools have subsequently acquired laptops through the 1-to-1 state contract, and other high schools have found ways to fund equipment purchases on their own.

A lot of the high schools have invested heavily in mobile carts. Dr. Muir explains (ibid.) that state financial challenges have forced Maine to delay expanding the program to high schools:

> Although carts are a good first step toward 1-to-1, there are significant differences between the two, with benefits of 1-to-1 which aren't realized with a cart program.

1-TO-1 ADVICE

Dr. Muir's advice to other schools or districts considering a 1-to-1 program is unequivocal: "You have to do it! I think [a laptop program] better meets the needs of this generation of students. Do it 1-to-1, not on carts" (ibid.). He's not a believer in mobile laptop carts because they tend to become just another form of computer lab. With laptop carts, there's no chance for spontaneous or serendipitous learning because the computers need to be scheduled in advance.

Other lessons cited by Dr. Muir include the following:

▶ Pay attention to teaching and learning first (**E** for educators *and* education).

▶ Leadership is vital. Leaders need to set a vision for teaching and learning. Appropriate polices need to be created.

▶ Find sustainable funding systems. This includes good partnerships, educational organizations, grants, and so forth.

▶ Be sure to support your teachers. Every school needs to have a technology integrator, someone who focuses solely on integrating technology into the classroom.

▶ Professional development is an ongoing process, not a one-shot deal. It needs to be adapted in response to the successes and challenges experienced by teachers and the institution as a whole.

▶ Students and teachers need complete, 24/7 access to technology. It needs to work when they need it to work.

▶ Infrastructure, logistics, insurance, acceptable use policies—all must be addressed in the planning process.

▶ Laptops need to be at home and not just at school.

Manchester offers similar advice (personal communication, November 23, 2005):

> Definitely talk to people who have been involved in [similar laptop] projects. Don't just take the RFP [and buy hardware]—go and visit, and be clear about why you want to establish a laptop program. Set a purpose. Purpose drives what happens.

She cautions (ibid.), however, that vision and purpose must also be discussed at the building level. Successful implementation of any program depends on the community in which it takes place, so each community must establish its purpose first. These communities are not just internal:

> Another example of [community] inclusion is the Digital Media Group—an organization of content providers in Maine that includes Public Broadcasting, the Maine Historical Society, Northeast Historic Film, the Portland Museum of Art, Maine libraries, and other organizations.

In Maine, these learning communities operate for students as well. Student tech teams called iTeams help teachers with technical support and lend a student voice to the project. One group has even developed a video to help educate other student tech teams. Once a year, these teams gather for an annual conference to share and plan, just as teachers gather regularly to share and plan: "Students are at the heart of this project. It's the same [model] for students, [finding out] what works and what doesn't work," Manchester says (ibid.).

Both Dr. Muir and Manchester believe strongly that educators today have a moral obligation to provide their students with access to digital educational tools because their learning styles and needs are fundamentally different from those of earlier generations. While for most adults the standard medium of instruction and information sharing is text, the natural learning medium of the millennials is video. Adults are uni-taskers, but millennials are natural multitaskers and shouldn't be forced to adopt the learning behaviors of their teachers. If educators ignore these fundamental differences, they risk irrelevancy in the minds of the students they are hoping to teach. As Dr. Seymour Papert says (2003), students don't mind hard, they mind boring. Motivated and engaged learners are not bored, and the experience of the MLTI tells us that providing students with laptops can be a key to better engagement.

ILLINOIS' I-CONNECT PROGRAM FOLLOWS IN MAINE'S FOOTSTEPS

Illinois lieutenant governor Pat Quinn is a podcaster; you can subscribe to his posts from the state of Illinois' Web site. It's not surprising, then, that starting September 2006 this tech-savvy leader wants to provide every seventh-grader in Illinois with a laptop. That would mean a total initial deployment of 170,000 laptops, making it the largest laptop program in the country. Funding for this program, known as i-Connect, is the major stumbling block. The original plan calls for funding the program through a tax loophole, but that's still being debated as this book goes to press. For more information on this ambitious 1-to-1 initiative, go to http://standingupforillinois.org/connect/downloads/iConnect-Facts.pdf.

The State of Michigan

Like Maine, the driving force for Michigan's laptop initiative was a visionary politician. In 2002, Rick Johnson, speaker of the house in Michigan's Legislature, was invited to visit Microsoft's and Apple Computer's corporate campuses. He also visited both Maine and Henrico County, Virginia, to learn more about their 1-to-1 programs.

Johnson was motivated to make these trips out of concern that Michigan wasn't doing enough to help those students who needed it most. He was looking for answers in education technology. He was particularly impressed that Henrico County students often congregated in their high school parking lot on Saturdays to access their wireless network. He saw the potential benefits for students in his own state and went to work to find funding for a pilot program called Learning Without Limits.

Working with fellow state legislators, Johnson pieced together a program with $3.5 million in state funding and $6 million in federal funding (Wireless Developer Network, www.wirelessdevnet.com/newswire-less/aug302002.html, downloaded January 2, 2006). David Seitz, one of the authors of the No Child Left Behind legislation, also got involved in the early stages. He used his contacts with industry and the Bush administration to help get this initiative off the ground. At the time, Seitz was serving as deputy director and policy development coordinator for the Michigan House Republican Policy Office. The initial project was tied to NCLB and offered laptops to low-income districts that had at least one school on the NCLB school improvement list.

Bruce Montgomery was subsequently hired to be executive director of an expanded program, renamed the Freedom to Learn Program. Montgomery graciously agreed to be interviewed about the planning and execution of Michigan's laptop program, and his answers form the basis of this profile.

The program began with a demonstration phase in which eight different 1-to-1 programs were funded. Participating schools were allowed to choose either laptops or handhelds, but the devices had to be wireless. A total of 8,000 students participated in these eight programs, and about half were using handhelds. All the major hardware vendors were represented, including IBM, Gateway, Apple, Hewlett-Packard, Palm, and Dell. The focus of this demonstration phase, however, was not on the vendors but on the devices them- selves. In the end, laptops were preferred by both teachers and students because they better supported the types of things students and teachers wanted to accomplish and learn.

Montgomery was then faced with the challenge of turning these pilot programs into something that would be scalable for the entire state. Rather than allowing each district to select a provider and then trying to manage this at the state level, Montgomery felt it would be best if the state could identify and choose a single vendor who would offer a single solution package. This kind of large-scale procurement is also something the state does on a regular basis for other resources. Consequently, Montgomery and the state Legislature proposed a laptop procurement program with three key stipulations:

1. The state would authorize the funds to do this as a laptop program and nothing else.

2. The state would set aside a full 25% of the total funding for professional development for teachers.

3. The state would choose a single solution provider to handle the entire program.

The media got wind of this proposal and initially projected that Michigan would either choose Dell or Apple. Instead, after reviewing all proposals, Michigan selected Hewlett-Packard based on the selection criteria in the state's RFP, which included the quality of the laptop device, support for wireless networking, the maintenance and warranty agreement, support services to schools, content and curriculum resources, and professional development. Michigan's procurement decision was based on the delivery and maintenance of a complete education package for less than $275 per student per year, a total of $1,100 per student for the program's initial 4 years (B. Montgomery, personal communication, January 4, 2006).

Cautionary Tale

Cobb County, Georgia

Cobb County, Georgia, announced a major laptop initiative in May 2005, but it was stopped by a court order just before rollout in July 2005 (www.macworld.com/news/2005/07/29/cobbcounty/index.php, downloaded January 2, 2006). At issue was how public money was being spent and how the vendor contract had been awarded. The Superior Court judge in Cobb County decided district administrators hadn't adequately informed taxpayers how sales tax money was to be used for the program. Cobb County's superintendent resigned, multiple subpoenas were served, and a grand jury has been impaneled for a full investigation to see if any laws were broken. That investigation is ongoing, but what's certain at this point is that Cobb County doesn't have laptops for its 63,000 students as planned. The moral of the story: always communicate thoroughly with all your constituents.

THE ADVISORY COUNCIL (P FOR PLANNING)

Michigan put together an advisory council in 2003. The first year, the advisory council included representatives from every major hardware manufacturer. These early meetings proved frustrating and unhelpful, however, because they were more about overt and covert sales pitches than about moving the program forward. Each vendor wanted to direct the program its own way, and this proved untenable.

The makeup of the advisory council was subsequently changed in the second year to refocus the discussion on education rather than hardware. Meetings included technology coordinators, curriculum specialists, and educational association representatives such as the Michigan Association of Computer Users in Learning. The Michigan State Department of Education was also at the table.

Montgomery felt it was important to have representatives from all three areas—education, industry, and government—to ensure that no perspective was being overlooked. Since the Freedom to Learn Program was taking resources and Title II funds that individual districts would otherwise have had free control over, Montgomery wanted to make sure that the program represented a broad-based consensus on what would really work and what could be implemented consistently throughout the state. The advisory council continues to receive feedback today, Montgomery says, from "a cross-section of organizations, especially the Michigan Department of Education, Hewlett-Packard and its partners, and the participating school districts" (ibid.).

PROGRAM GOALS

The Freedom to Learn Program's principal goal is to help individuals develop into self-sustaining, self-directed learners. Montgomery emphasizes, however, that this goal doesn't mean to disparage the role of teachers. Instead, the program seeks to give teachers the tools they need to reach their students more effectively. Once they get some experience teaching with laptops, he says, teachers realize they no longer have to be the dictator of all learning in the classroom. When they get beyond the fear of losing power over what and how students learn, they find that laptops free them up to be learning facilitators and student advocates rather than the dreaded (and thus often ignored) authority figure typified by the "sage on the stage" archetype. Montgomery says (personal communication, August 9, 2005):

> We don't wave a flag around, but we are not shy about what we hope [to achieve]—we are hoping that this works so well that all educators will begin to ask for [laptops] and schools will figure out how to integrate them at many levels. It's not just a fad.

Like Maine's, Michigan's laptop program was motivated in part by economic self-interest, with leaders looking to produce highly computer-literate graduates who would be attractive to high tech employers. But improving student achievement has always been a primary goal as well. This is no easy task, as Montgomery points out (personal communication, January 4, 2006):

> If you are just measuring the effectiveness of the programs based on standardized tests, what educators fear is that the whole notion of critical thinking, independent learning, and the construction of new understanding will be ignored. These progressive goals have to be accommodated even while schools and districts hew to the accountability line. Schools must look to improve student achievement on standardized tests, but they also must keep students engaged. I am of the mind that you can do both with a 1-to-1 teaching and learning program that is student-centered. That's what we have to do to move these programs forward— show that they can lead to improved student performance while at the same time supporting project-based, constructivist learning activities.

HOW LAPTOPS ARE USED IN MICHIGAN SCHOOLS

Michigan evaluated its Freedom to Learn Program in March 2005 and published an internal progress report that looks at the early impact of the Freedom to Learn Program on student learning and engagement. The report notes statistically significant improvements in standardized test scores, including improved reading and math scores at Bendle Middle School and Bear Lake Schools. The study also reports fewer discipline issues and increased attendance in school.

The report also includes anecdotal stories describing how teachers are using laptops to encourage collaborative and group work. Teachers and students are using the laptops to enhance writing assignments, perform virtual science labs, analyze data with spreadsheets, research on the Web, and create more professional PowerPoint presentations. In all content areas, laptops are being used to support higher order thinking, collaborative and cooperative learning, and student inquiry.

The teachers quoted in the report describe richer and deeper projects, more engaged students, and opportunities to work in ways that would not be possible without computers. One teacher says laptops have had a transformative effect on her classroom: "Because of our laptops, my students were able to do all of their research, writing, and publishing right here in our classroom...No one had to wait for a computer, everyone was on task, no one was disruptive, and everyone participated" (ibid.).

LOOKING AT THE PROGRAM TODAY, AND PLANNING FOR TOMORROW

Michigan now has 22,000 students using laptops. The state is monitoring the program in conjunction with site-based monitors. Individual districts have different policies on whether or not students are allowed to take their computers home. In areas with higher crime rates, this can be dangerous. Hewlett-Packard and Microsoft have stepped in to help with the school-to-home issue by setting up a centralized server so that Freedom to Learn participants can use any Internet connection to access their school files and applications. Thus, they don't have to take their laptop home with them.

For professional development, Michigan has constructed a number of demonstration and advisory sites. The people involved with these sites are "the practitioners that I listen to now," says Montgomery. Michigan manages the program like a business, with planning tools, timeframes, and assessments: "We use both formative (ongoing) and summative evaluation tools to measure success in the classroom and across the state. Our classroom assessment tools allow us to measure our progress school by school and student by student" (ibid.).

As for sustaining the program into the future, the Freedom to Learn Program must go back to the state each year to renew funding. So far, both houses of the state government have voted to continue funding the program. Montgomery says the program will continue with or without the funding. However, he also says the plan is to build a model for school-based funding that would enable individual schools to fund their own laptop programs using money from a combination of sources. This will require total-cost-of-ownership studies, which are currently underway. Montgomery doesn't think it's reasonable to expect the state to fund the entire program year after year; the combination of funding sources will always vary. In the future, the state may match title funds with Freedom to Learn funds, thus combining state and federal sources. He hopes Michigan's program will eventually lead to a national 1-to-1 movement that will have broad-ranging support. He says (ibid.):

> Recently the program received start-up private funding to initiate an institute to help other
> states and large school districts plan and prepare their own 1-to-1 programs. It is inevitable
> that technology will someday be in the hands of every student on an anytime, anywhere basis.
> With our partners from Maine, Texas, Virginia, and other locations, we would like to help
> school districts—especially high need urban schools—get ready to efficiently and effectively
> plan and launch successful 1-to-1 programs. We have learned a lot over the past few years

and want to help others avoid repeating our mistakes while making use of our lessons learned and best practices. Sustainability will continue to be an issue until businesses, educational stakeholders, parents, and taxpayers see the value of this program. That is the challenge.

Chapter 4

WHAT 1-TO-1 CAN MEAN FOR STUDENTS, TEACHERS, AND SCHOOLS

Introduction

THE SCHOOLS, DISTRICTS, AND STATES profiled in the first three chapters provide plenty of anecdotal evidence about the benefits 1-to-1 laptops can bring to students and teachers alike. But what about formal evidence: what quantitative or qualitative research has been done on the benefits of 1-to-1 computing?

While formal research is still scanty and fragmentary—largely because 1-to-1 programs are so new—some compelling studies have been published recently which suggest that 1-to-1 can have a strongly beneficial impact on a variety of measures of student performance. This chapter will summarize the most pertinent findings from these studies as well as the lessons learned and insights gleaned by the experts who have pioneered laptop initiatives.

Figure 4.1
Beaufort County students create mutimedia projects using their laptops.

What 1-to-1 Can Mean for Students

At the end of the day, the success of a 1-to-1 program must be measured by the ways and extent to which it improves student learning. Disregarding for the moment the politically charged debate over how best to measure student performance, we must keep in mind that if students don't gain something important from ubiquitous access to their own digital assistants, then a lot of time, energy, and money will have been wasted. In the end, all education reforms must be about students—how they learn and what they learn. This section summarizes the most important benefits to students when digital assistants are part of the learning mix.

1-TO-1 helps students improve their technology and information processing skills, preparing students for higher education and jobs in the technology-driven global economy

Students are natural explorers, unafraid to point and click and figure things out. But it's by getting students to go beyond familiar tasks and the easy-to-discover secrets of a particular program or Web resource that the true promise of technology can be realized. We must challenge them to tackle more advanced activities that require active collaboration and higher order thinking skills.

I once observed a student type the following search string into Google: "Vietnam War supplies Ho Chi Min Trail difficulty of getting." When he hit enter, he received a long list of unrelated documents on the Vietnam War: office supplies, Ho Chi Min City biking trails, and so forth. Wading through all these hits was clearly going to be a time-consuming—and possibly useless—task, so the student promptly pronounced to me that there was "nothing out there" on his topic.

This example reveals that no matter how quick and accessible the best technology tools are, technology users still need to learn how to use them effectively and thoughtfully if they're to support critical thinking and problem solving. This kind of learning can only take place over time and through frequent use. It will not happen if students get only 15 minutes on a computer every other week or so.

Laptops enable students to take their digital assistants everywhere and use them for all kinds of learning activities: writing, sorting, organizing, experimenting, linking, making mistakes that no one sees, and so on. Computer labs—and even laptops on carts—cannot give students the 24/7 access they need to become operationally adept with digital resources.

Having a digital assistant at one's fingertips means increased opportunities to hone crucial technology skills. Howard Levin observes (personal communication, December 22, 2004) that student technology skills improved significantly across the board when laptops were introduced at The Urban School in San Francisco:

> One of the overwhelming successes [of the laptop program] is that it has dramatically increased computer technology confidence among everyone...This provides an enormous advantage because it enables students to be far ahead of other students who are not as tech savvy. [These laptop-using] kids don't even think they're especially tech savvy because it is such a normal part of their lives.

Independent educational research firm Rockman *et al* (2000, p. iv) compared students who have laptops with those who don't and found laptop-using students were far more fluid users of technology:

> Laptop students consistently show deeper and more flexible uses of technology than their Non-Laptop matched groups.

Administrators at the Athens (Georgia) Academy report (Hill & Reeves, 2004, p. 43) that students with laptops were far more productive and efficient in their use of common applications:

The data indicates that there is an increased use of e-mail, Web browsers, Word, PowerPoint and Excel for productivity for both teachers and learners. Further, the data indicates that teachers and learners have realized that the laptops make getting schoolwork completed easier and more efficient.

The students have also reported growth in their perceptions of personal abilities with technology…This was not the case in Year One when many Middle School girls reported feeling like their peers knew more than they did. (ibid., p. 16)

Barbara Catenaci, the education technology development specialist at Beaufort County (South Carolina) School District, also marvels at how much more productive students become when they regularly use a laptop to complete schoolwork (personal communication, November 15, 2004):

They use the computers less as the years [go] on. It's because they [are] better at it. If you ask how much time they are spending at a computer, you will see it. The first time they did an Excel spreadsheet it took a lot longer.

1-TO-1 provides crucial support for constructivist instructional practices and motivates students to become self-directed learners

With a digital assistant for use at school and home, real time is available for students to go beyond teacher- or textbook-generated lessons and activities and seek out their own sources of information and learning. Laptops are a great enabling tool for project-based learning and other constructivist practices. Administrators of Project Hiller—a laptop program for ninth-graders in Union City, New Jersey—point to this as a major benefit of 1-to-1 access:

In one example, a ninth-grade [laptop user]…was involved in a class project to do field research and write about the impact of different inventions on society. On his own, he and his partner—who were studying the impact of the automobile—distributed surveys over the Internet to contacts in Miami and rural Tennessee so that they could compare trends…The teacher was pleased not only with the initiative but that the duo asked if they could exceed the 10-page limit for their report. (Light, McDermott, & Honey, 2002, p. 24)

Alex Inman was impressed with how quickly students at Whitfield School in St. Louis developed into active, self-directed learners when provided with laptops (personal communication, December 15, 2004):

It was great seeing students go from fumbling kids who could not use the tool to becoming curriculum designers, asking what is it that you want to accomplish, and fitting what they did to the overall goal.

A seventh-grade parent in Maine reports that her son's whole approach to learning has changed since he was given a laptop:

Simply put, my seventh-grade son is loving his laptop…[He's] done virtually *all* of his homework since November on this machine, and in general enjoyed every discovery he's made…He feels good about his accomplishments in a way I haven't seen for the past 7 years. He's learning more material, and he's learning it faster. He's excited about learning. Bravo!!! (Lane, 2003, p. 18)

A student participant in Project Hiller describes quite succinctly the changes she noted in herself:

> I can do whatever I want and teach myself...before, I was clueless. (Light, McDermott, & Honey, 2002, p. 23)

Teachers know what a difference student motivation can make in the classroom. 1-to-1 empowers students and gives them a more active role in choosing what and how they study, resulting in better study behavior and improved learning outcomes. As researcher Mel Levine points out in his book *A Mind at a Time* (2002, p. 263):

> Success nourishes motivation and motivation makes further success more likely...The neurodevelopmental systems require constant exercise if they are to stay in good shape. Such persistent use is partly dependent upon motivation to learn, that is, a willingness to absorb and endure the risks that go with new and ever more demanding brain challenges.

1-TO-1 helps students stay organized and on track with their schoolwork

Anytime access to all learning materials and assignments helps students stay organized and study more efficiently. These benefits go beyond preventing lost homework and keeping track of grades: students can use their computers to customize their personal learning environment, making connections and organizing the parts and processes in a way that makes the most sense to them. This is one of the most powerful educational benefits of a personal digital assistant: everything is easily accessible, personally organized, and instantly available—anytime and anywhere.

In their study of laptop programs, Rockman *et al* (2000, p. 61) found that laptop-using students almost universally felt that they were more organized and kept track of their schoolwork better with the help of their digital assistants:

> **Organization:** Laptop students felt that computers helped them keep their work organized; they felt they didn't lose their work when it was all on their own computers.

Having everything they're studying and learning in one place, organized in a way that makes sense to them, is powerful and motivating for students. Bill Ivey describes (personal communication, February 8, 2005) what a difference this has made at Stoneleigh-Burnham School in Greenfield, Massachusetts, the all-girls' school where he works:

> I think maybe the greatest success has been the ability to allow kids to be working at their own level, always moving forward, using their time differently depending on their own learning styles and needs, staying organized and on topic in a way that would be much more difficult without the laptops.

A Peck School seventh-grader typifies the reaction of many laptop-using students who compare 1-to-1 favorably with the hassles of sharing a computer at school and at home:

> Last year, I found it much more difficult to do my computer-related homework, because I would have to go to a whole other computer and put in my password, search frantically for history papers, and English essays that had gotten lost in all the other materials. This year, I just turn my laptop on, and everything I need is right in front of me. (Livingston, 2004, p. 78)

Another Peck School student elaborated on his method for keeping track of notes, class materials, software, and other electronic information:

> My homework, class notes are on the laptop. I take all the old work from those chapters and put them in a folder for chapter 1, 2, and so on. All of the schedules I have to have, the syllabus for science... I have a folder for extra stuff that I need to keep but can't categorize, another folder for software... It's just easier for me. (Livingston, 2004, p. 76)

What 1-to-1 Can Mean for Teachers

A teacher's work extends far beyond the dismissal bell each day. Some of it involves staying in the classroom after students have left, and some of it's done from home on nights, weekends, holidays, vacations, and over the summer. Just as students can organize their work, customize it according to their own learning styles, and complete it with more depth and better resources, so, too, is the vital work of teachers made easier and better when they have ubiquitous access to a digital assistant. A laptop can help a teacher with myriad needs: planning, instructing, communicating, revising, researching, analyzing, reflecting, writing, presenting, publishing, recording, calculating, and a lot more.

Teachers are professionals charged with the life-altering mission of educating our youth. Providing laptops to teachers is not just about having them become more comfortable with computers and technology. It's about giving them the best tools available to succeed in their socially critical work with our country's next generation.

1-TO-1 can help teachers become more adept and confident in using education technology for planning, teaching, and communication

Surveys of laptop-using teachers and interviews with laptop leaders indicate that teachers become more comfortable with technology and more adept at its use when they're provided a laptop computer and teach in a laptop environment.

Rockman *et al* (2004, pp. 24, 36, 43) spent 3 years studying laptop schools that were part of the Microsoft/Toshiba Anytime Anywhere Learning initiative. When comparing data they compiled on teachers who used laptops versus those who didn't, they found big differences in each group's overall use of education technology:

> Laptop teachers use computers far more often in a wider variety of learning activities than non-laptop peers. Their students use computers more often for data analysis (77 percent vs. 5 percent), presentations (59 percent vs. 16 percent), writing (72 percent vs. 21 percent) and research (85 percent vs. 35 percent)... Laptop teachers also have greater confidence in using technology tools like word processing, e-mail, and the Internet.

Researchers at WestEd (2002, p. 2) are similarly categorical about how regular use of computers can help teachers become more effective at integrating technology into the classroom:

> For technology to become a core component of teachers' instructional repertoire, they not only need familiarity with equipment, but—more important—they need to see and practice the most productive ways of using it to support learning.

Administrators at Athens Academy found (Hill & Reeves, 2004, p. 32) that teachers' use of technology expanded significantly when they were provided with a laptop:

> Another area of change has occurred in teachers' and learners' perspectives related to their individual abilities with the technology. The data indicate significant growth in use of tools by both teachers and learners in the Middle and Upper School. Teachers reported higher degrees of confidence in their technological abilities. Further, many teachers have expanded the tools they are using and are exploring how other tools might impact their classroom practices.

1-TO-1 can provide teachers with ready access to a whole world of curricular resources that encourage and support the development of richer lessons

The enrichment of resources available to students is something all good teachers want. When I was in school, I loved getting a shiny new textbook and would peruse its pages with awe, wondering what worlds it would help me explore. That same excitement and enthusiasm can be multiplied many times over when students gain access to the endless supply of well-designed learning resources and authentic materials available online.

Administrators at the Athens Academy found (ibid., p. 43) laptops encouraged teachers to incorporate online resources more readily into their classrooms:

> The data show teachers are increasing use of the laptops to enable them to bring real resources into their classrooms easily and in a "right on time" fashion.

Likewise, evaluators of Maine's statewide laptop program report that teachers readily expand their curricular horizons when given a laptop to use in the classroom:

> Teachers feel the laptops are very helpful in developing integrated lessons and extending learning. In many teacher interviews, teachers have described how they have been able to locate materials and information to use in developing interdisciplinary units—to help students see connections between different pieces of information and knowledge...[Typical comments from teachers include the following:] "The laptop is such an integral part of all my management routines that I can't imagine life without it. I use the Web to find rich teaching resources." (Sargent, 2003/April, p. 11)

> Teachers are seeing the greatest impact of the MLTI on their work in planning and presenting lessons, creating integrated lessons, and creating assignments. Teachers reported that having the laptop as a tool enables them, in many cases, to expand their own knowledge and increase their efficiency. (Silvernail & Harris, 2003/March, p. 10)

Beaufort School District (Stevenson, 1999/November, p. ii) reports that finding classroom resources is one of the primary uses that district-supplied laptops are put to:

> Teachers personally used the computers most often for lesson planning or research.

1-TO-1 can help teachers communicate more frequently and effectively with students, parents, and colleagues

So much of learning is about communication. Teachers continually check for understanding in a variety of ways: directly querying their students, giving tests and quizzes, assigning reports, asking students to present their findings. All are modes of communication through which new learning and understanding take place.

Providing teachers and students with 24/7 access to computers expands and reinforces their ability to communicate. Questions and ideas can be composed, reviewed, revised, revisited, and submitted more easily and frequently, expanding the opportunities for learning.

Research from Maine (Sargent, 2003/April, p. 7) points to how teachers have increased their communication with one another now that they all have laptops:

> One of the most frequent uses of the laptops by teachers is in communicating with colleagues. Approximately 55% of the teachers surveyed reported that they use their laptop to communicate with colleagues at least a few times a week.

Administrators at the Athens Academy also noted an increase in the ease and frequency of communication among their laptop-using faculty and students (Hill & Reeves, 2004, p. 42, 52):

> Teachers and learners are using the laptops for enhanced communication between themselves and others. Teachers reported that working with teammates and colleagues in general has been enhanced with the ease in communication brought about by Internet tools, especially e-mail... Teachers also indicated an increase in the use of e-mail for communicating with parents and students.

Howard Levin reports (personal communication, November 15, 2004) that a Spanish teacher at The Urban School found having a laptop made a huge difference in his ability to provide students with appropriate language input outside the normal boundaries of the classroom and class assignments:

> The key, the catalyst, was he has been able to extend oral and aural language practice through e-mail. This demonstrated a real way to extended language discussion with students beyond the classroom.

What 1-to-1 Can Mean for Schools

In 2002, at the National Educational Computing Conference in Seattle, I gave a presentation about Peck School's laptop program. Just before my presentation, I listened to one about Maine's laptop initiative. I was eager to learn what they'd experienced in their program's first year. The speaker told us the major benefit was improved school attendance. After the session, several in the room expressed disappointment in that limited result: "Is that it? Just better attendance?"

Evidence has mounted for a variety of other instructional and student performance benefits in the years since—in Maine as well as in other 1-to-1 programs. However, we should not discount the importance of this very simple but profound improvement: when students are given their own laptops, their school attendance invariably improves. Clearly, this means that laptop-using students want to come to school more. In the long run, this is bound to lead to increases in student performance as measured by standardized test scores, graduation rates, and career success outside of school.

1-TO-1 can improve both student attendance and school enrollment

Solid evidence has emerged from multiple sources that students given laptops tend to be more involved and interested in what they learn and are thus less likely to stay home (Lane, 2003/April, p. 2). Since that first year, Maine has continued to see a significant increase in attendance rates:

> Preliminary findings suggest that since the implementation of the laptop program, student engagement and attendance has increased and the classroom atmosphere has shifted, including more student/teacher and student/student collaboration.

Fewer absences have also been reported in Manatee County (Florida), which has a laptop program in 22 classrooms from elementary through high school (Barrios, 2004/March 22, p. 2):

> Absences have declined nearly 40% among students with laptops.

Administrators of Project Hiller report not only an improvement in student attendance, but also an increase in the number of high-achieving students enrolling in public schools (Light, McDermott, & Honey, 2002/May, p. 2):

> The possibility of participation in Project Hiller encouraged high performing eighth-grade students to stay in the public school system. In the year prior to Project Hiller (1997–98), Union Hill enrolled just 38 ninth-grade honors students, while in 1998–99, the first year of the program, Union Hill drew 44 freshman students into its honors program. In the second and third year of the project, Union Hill admitted 59 and 55 students into the ninth-grade honors program respectively, representing a 25 percent increase from 1998 in the number of high achieving eighth-graders choosing to enroll at the high school.

1-TO-1 can improve student performance in all curricular areas

Longitudinal data on the effects of 1-to-1 access on standardized test scores and other measures of student performance are still fragmentary and limited at this point. However, research is beginning to reveal that ubiquitous access to technology can have a profound effect on student achievement.

A recent study of 259 laptop-using students at Harvest Park Middle School in Pleasanton, California, shows that students in 1-to-1 classrooms had higher scores than their non-laptop-using peers on standardized tests for English language arts, mathematics, and writing. They also had higher overall GPAs (Gulek & Demirtas, 2005).

The study also echoes previous research that shows students in 1-to-1 classrooms "spend more time involved in collaborative work, participate in more project-based instruction, produce writing of higher quality and greater length, gain increased access to information, improve research analysis skills, and spend more time doing homework on computers" (Gulek & Demirtas, 2005, abstract). The Harvest Park middle-schoolers, like students in other 1-to-1 programs, "report a greater reliance on active learning strategies, readily engage in problem solving and critical thinking, and consistently show deeper and more flexible uses of technology than students without individual laptops" (ibid.).

While these are promising results, the study is careful to point out that these improvements did not appear immediately. Any new technology or curricular reform has a learning curve, and schools should expect an adjustment period when implementing a 1-to-1 program. In the case of Harvest Park, that adjustment period was about one semester. By the end of the first year, "laptop students showed significantly higher achievement in nearly all measures after one year in the program" (ibid.).

As reforms go, this is remarkably fast and significant improvement, especially given that other education technology initiatives have had little direct impact on student test scores. Interestingly, the sixth-graders at Harvest Park seem to have demonstrated greater improvement than older students. Could this be because they're at the ideal developmental stage to take on these new technologies and approaches? More research is needed to isolate differential factors, but this result reflects what I have seen at The Peck School: younger students seem to embrace new resources and technologies more readily and enthusiastically than older students.

Gulek and Demirtas (2005, p. 29) cite other research in trying to explain why writing scores in particular seem to have improved so much among laptop-using students:

> The findings related to writing are consistent with results of a recent meta-analysis of studies that investigated the effect of computers on student writing (Goldberg, Russell & Cook, 2003). This meta-analysis found that students who use computers when learning to write are not only more engaged and motivated in their writing, but also produce work that is of greater length and higher quality, especially at the secondary level.

Given laptop-using students' enhanced ability to compose, revise, edit, and publish their writing, it makes sense that they spend more time with writing assignments and produce better work.

Other pertinent findings (Gulek & Demirtas, 2005, p. 7, 13):

> QUESTION: Does the laptop program have an impact on students' grade point average?

> ANSWER: Results indicate that Harvest Park Middle School students in the Laptop Immersion Program attained higher GPAs than non-participating students in their respective grades. The greatest difference was observed in sixth grade GPAs.

> QUESTION: Does the laptop program have an impact on students' end-of-course grades?

> ANSWER: Results indicate that there is a substantial difference between laptop and non-laptop students in terms of their end-of-course grades. A notably higher percentage of laptop students attained A grades and a significantly lower percentage attained F grades in their English and mathematics courses. The largest difference between percent of laptop and non-laptop students obtaining A grades was in seventh grade English and the smallest difference was in eighth grade mathematics.

> QUESTION: Does the laptop program have an impact on students' standardized test scores?

> ANSWER: Results indicate that a considerably higher proportion of laptop students scored at or above the national average in both the language and mathematics portions of the California Achievement Test sixth Edition Survey Form (CAT/6 Survey) across all grade levels. The largest difference in NRT outcomes occurred between current sixth grade laptop

and non-laptop students in math, and current eighth grade students in total language, when they were tested at the end of their first year enrollment in the laptop program.

Additional statistical evidence for the benefits of 1-to-1 can be found in the Education Development Center's 3-year study of Project Hiller (Light, McDermott, & Honey, 2002/May, pp. 1–2):

> Standardized test scores rose significantly for Project Hiller students across all tracks. Analysis of ninth-grade scores for Cohort 1 indicated no difference between participants and their peers prior to Project Hiller; however, by years 2 and 3 of the project, participating students scored significantly higher than their non-Project Hiller peers. For example, within the honors track in specific regard to math scores, Project Hiller students scored 414.05 on the New Jersey State High School Proficiency Test (HSPT) versus 396.14 scored by their non-Hiller peers.

Supporters of Michigan's Freedom to Learn (FTL) initiative credit the program with improving grades, motivation, and discipline. Early returns from Michigan's statewide 1-to-1 program also reveal a strong positive influence on student test scores. Results from the January/February 2005 administration of the Michigan Educational Assessment Program (MEAP) test show that students in 1-to-1 laptop programs outperform their peers by a wide margin (Solomon, 2005, p. 4):

▶ In Bendle Middle School, the percentage of seventh-graders who scored "proficient" in reading increased from 29% to 41%, while the percentage of eighth-graders who scored "proficient" in math rose from 31% to 63%.

▶ In Leland Middle School, the percentage of students who scored "proficient" on the MEAP writing test rose from 53% to 84%—compared to a statewide average of 53%.

▶ Across the Eastern Upper Peninsula ISD, in just one year, the percentage of students who scored "proficient" in science increased from 68% to 80%, while the percentage of students who scored "proficient" in math increased from 57% to 67%.

Bruce Montgomery, executive director of the FTL program, points out the significance of these early returns (ibid.)

> Usually, such overwhelmingly positive results like this aren't seen for three or four years out. Clearly, FTL is doing what it is designed to do for our school children—enhance student learning and achievement in core academic subjects.

Mike Hester, principal of Hays (Kansas) High School, reports improved test scores since implementing a 1-to-1 laptop program (available at www.apple.com/education/k12/onetoone/classroom.html):

> This year our math and reading test scores were up 12 to 17 percent over AYP (Adequate Yearly Progress), and we met the standard of excellence in social studies and science, scoring over the 80th percentile in both.

1-TO-1 improves the home-to-school connection

People who know I've been researching this subject often ask me what the real benefits of laptops are, emphasizing "real" as if they expect to hear nothing but vague promises and platitudes. Education technology skeptics point to the expense involved in acquiring enough laptops for a 1-to-1 program, not to mention the training, support, infrastructure changes, and curricular restructuring required. They cite previous failed school reform projects, relate anecdotes of students using laptops merely as powerful music-downloading devices, talk about studies on the difficulty of integrating technology into teaching, and on and on.

To these folks, my typical one word answer is always "Homework." When students have their own laptop, their homework is always with them. The dog can't eat it, it can't be accidentally tossed in the trash, and it's not likely to be forgotten on the bus or dropped in a puddle on the way home from school. All of the resources that students need to complete their homework go with them: online resources and references, databases and spreadsheets, e-books and other primary source material, and so on. It's all in one place and easily transportable from school to home and back again.

Improvements in student homework and the home-to-school connection are a consistent refrain among 1-to-1 leaders nationwide. Here are just two representative anecdotes:

> He can do homework in waiting rooms, on long car rides, on his mother's boring shopping trips—anywhere! He feels good about his accomplishments in a way I haven't seen for the past 7 years. He's learning more material, and he's learning it faster. (Silvernail & Harris, 2003/March, p. 30)

> According to one principal, students who were reluctant to do homework became more willing to do it once it was on the computer. Students who did not have excellent handwriting skills could produce neat work, and in general, students had the ability to produce more professional-looking products. (Zucker & McGhee, 2005/February, p. 16)

Conclusion

According to the studies and school reports examined for this chapter, students who use laptops are more motivated and empowered, are more organized and engaged learners, attend school more regularly, advance their knowledge and understanding of technology, and become constructors and designers of information and ideas. Speaking from the vantage point of someone who's been an education technologist for more than a decade, I daresay this seems exactly like what we've been trying to accomplish all along. Don't be afraid to give power to the students.

Part Two

BUILDING A SUCCESSFUL 1-TO-1 PROGRAM

MANY THINGS NEED TO BE CONSIDERED once the decision is made to introduce a laptop program. The first and usually most important step is thoughtful, in-depth planning that aligns with both the school's mission and district and state standards. Planning is critical to a program's success and sustainability, yet it's often where shortcuts are made. Even when it's done well, the planning process is sometimes ended too quickly, and the program isn't steered in a structured way. Chapters 5 and 6 will help you ensure that all aspects of your new program have been considered and planned for.

Implementation is also a challenging process. Schools accustomed to running a wired network with desktop computers that never move from classrooms or labs can sometimes be unpleasantly surprised when hundreds of new users on wireless, mobile laptops are suddenly part of the mix. To avoid network meltdown, it's important to pay close attention to implementation issues and take advantage of the lessons learned by other 1-to-1 schools. Chapter 7 is full of helpful tips to reduce implementation headaches.

Previewing the Chapters

Chapter 5 examines all aspects of planning a 1-to-1 laptop program: forming and staffing a planning committee, getting multiple stakeholders involved, documenting the work, choosing among platform options, determining infrastructure needs and network capacities, and so forth. The chapter also looks at the importance of ongoing evaluation as the program moves forward, to ensure that it develops in the ways envisioned by the planning committee.

Chapter 6 looks at professional development for teachers. This is perhaps the single most crucial factor in the success of a 1-to-1 program. If teachers aren't committed to the program and comfortable with the technology, 1-to-1 laptops won't result in any significant improvement in student learning. Professional development is often overlooked or underfunded during the planning phase, so this chapter is a must-read for all program planners and administrators.

Chapter 7 covers many of the nitty-gritty logistical issues of implementing a laptop program: firewalls, virus protection and security, e-mail scanning, proxy servers, Internet filtering, passwords and privacy, network storage, backup, file sharing, updates, tech support, laptop cases, laptop storage, warranties and insurance, theft, and summer preparation for fall rollout. Interspersed throughout this chapter are sidebars from 1-to-1 pioneers describing how they've overcome these and similar logistical challenges.

Chapter 5
THE PLANNING PROCESS

Introduction

AS DISCUSSED PREVIOUSLY, one of the most essential components of all the successful laptop programs reviewed in this book is the planning (**P**) that took place before any laptops were purchased. Schools and districts differ in mission, instructional philosophy, teaching styles, demographics, and a myriad other factors. So, too, is the approach to planning 1-to-1 programs unique to each individual institution.

While I can't offer a surefire blueprint that will work for every school or district, I can identify a number of essential steps that will ensure your planning process is as effective and complete as it can be. These steps include taking adequate time to plan; bringing in multiple stakeholders; documenting all efforts; learning from other school or district laptop programs; making sure to consider all of the logistical challenges unique to a laptop program; and assessing progress along the way. This chapter will look at all these essential steps in the planning process.

> Many schools are spending large amounts of money on technology. Some are doing so without defining why they need technology in the first place. (Britto, Fish, & Throckmorton, 2002, p. 4)

Figure 5.1
Suffield Academy has one of the longest-running laptop programs in the country.

Planning: A Necessary but Complex Effort

1-to-1 laptops can become nothing more than a way for students to download and listen to music or take class notes when schools or districts neglect to plan thoughtfully and systematically. New programs can fail very quickly if leaders ignore the importance of

- formulating a vision, with buy-in from multiple constituencies;

- hiring and empowering visionary educational leaders;

- providing adequate tech support, infrastructure, and computer repair;

- informing teachers that meaningful use of laptops in the classroom is a school-wide expectation;

- providing continuous professional development for teachers; and

- evaluating the progress of the program on a regular basis.

Individuals involved in 1-to-1 programs are unanimous on the importance of planning:

> A plan would have been nice! We had [administrators] who made the decision to supply laptops to our [students]. It was so impromptu that the technology department didn't have any input as to how these should be implemented... We had no time set aside for staff development or maintenance issues and curriculum integration ideas... Some of the teachers do okay integrating the technology. Others are using [laptops] as expensive notepads. (Personal communication from an anonymous technology employee at a public school district, January 15, 2005)

Given the multiple stakeholders involved—parents, teachers, students, administrators, school board members, taxpayers, political officeholders, and hardware and software vendors— and the differing needs and agendas they bring to the table, adequate planning is especially crucial for a large-scale technology implementation such as 1-to-1 laptops. Planners must carefully consider the funding needed, not only for initial purchases and immediate expenses, but also for the program's long-term sustainability. They need to take into account the high expectations of parents, taxpayers, the school board, and local elected officials, expectations that can easily rise to a level that no program, no matter how successful, could possibly fulfill.

Media attention can "spin" a new laptop program in a way that will leave school and district officials scrambling to correct misinformation and community reactions that result from it. Stakeholders interested primarily in school performance and adequate yearly progress may demand immediate return on dollars and other resources spent on laptops by way of higher student test scores, which may take a couple of years to show up.

Adequate, thoughtful planning can keep a school or district from being broadsided by these and other challenges to 1-to-1 implementation.

A Technology Plan That Is Not Driven by Technology

Some schools formulate technology plans that seem strong on paper but on closer look are driven by nuts and bolts and not by a vision of what the plan hopes to accomplish. These plans read like a list of jargon—bandwidth, protocols, platform, architecture, servers, cabling, topology, hardware, and IP scheme. With this kind of technology plan, the *educational use* of all this technology takes a back seat to *network operations*. Schools whose technology plans are written solely by technology experts without educational expertise will have networks that run reliably, as well as e-mail and Internet access for everyone, but meaningful use of technology in the classroom will be missing from those plans.

This doesn't mean that network, software, and hardware descriptions don't belong in the plan; they do. But they shouldn't be the primary focus of the document. Hardware, software, and network capabilities are all *support structures* that exist to facilitate classroom projects, communication, and learning. Successful technology plans must be driven by educational needs and learning goals, not technical specifications.

Just as we've seen that laptop programs can be different things to different schools, a plan for 1-to-1 computing should be carefully aligned with the particular goals and mission of each individual school or district. Separating technology from teaching and learning, and not making it an integral part of your institution's mission and educational goals, will not get you where you need to be. Ubiquitous technology needs to be supported not only physically but philosophically as well.

The Planning Committee—Who, What, How, and What Happens Next?

First of all, be sure you have a strong leader for your laptop initiative. This may seem obvious, but sometimes schools or districts don't spend the time to hire, promote, and empower the right person to be in charge. This person is most likely your technology director and ideally has one foot in education and one foot in education technology. To know what a teacher goes through in implementing a new program or technology, it really helps to have been a teacher yourself, since this gives credence to your ideas and improves the planning and implementation process.

If your laptop leader has more of a technical background than an educational one, be sure the leader schedules regular classroom observations as well as talks with teachers about teaching. Investing in a course or two and reading about pedagogy is also important. Your leader must have the trust of the teachers on the front lines to move your program ahead successfully.

Next, decide who will be on the planning committee and who will chair it. Choose members carefully and wisely, but be sure to include representatives from across your constituency. Your planning committee will also be your "vision" committee, because this group will formulate, decide, detail, market, implement, oversee, and assess how the program is put into practice in your school or district. Where your program goes will depend on how this group steers it, as well as how they turn over to other people the various pieces of the puzzle. Given the self-effacing culture of many schools and districts, however, it may be a good idea to play down this "visioning" aspect of the committee—at least publicly. Many educators espouse a "praise the class, not the individual" approach in their classrooms, and that may be the right tone to set here, too.

When creating and tasking the planning committee, keep in mind the particular culture of your school or district:

- ▶ What are its underlying operative beliefs?

- ▶ What are unique factors that frame, enhance, and mold where the school has been and where it's going?

- ▶ What are the educational, age, and socioeconomic profiles of the students being taught?

- ▶ What factors are unchangeable in your community and constituency?

- ▶ What's the predominant instructional philosophy of your school or district?

- ▶ How have other change initiatives been addressed? Why were they successful or not successful?

- ▶ How has technology worked or not worked in the past in your school or district?

Some of this will be found in your mission statement, but most of it will not.

Understanding your culture and what works will help you prioritize your efforts. For instance, if wounds from past innovations still haven't healed, analyze them carefully and seek ways to ease this new transition. Always keep in mind that your planning committee is leading that change. Perhaps change isn't even a word your organization often uses. If not, it's doubly important that you look for guidance from the leadership experts and researchers who have studied change. As leadership expert Michael Fullan notes, "For better or for worse, change arouses emotions, and when emotions intensify, leadership is key" (Fullan, 2001, p. 1).

Perhaps you already have a technology committee. Many schools and districts do—or did. This may be the place to start. However, in the past, this type of committee is likely to have worked on implementing a computer lab or computer network, both of which are separate from the day-to-day work of most teachers. A 1-to-1 program is a very different thing, and requires an entirely new focus. 1-to-1 takes computers out of these dedicated spaces and distributes them throughout the school. As a consequence, your technology committee may need both new ideas and new people to make it work for 1-to-1.

It's always a good idea to keep group and individual dynamics in mind. Kousez and Posner (1995, pp. 13–14) talk about "leading from the heart," an approach to leadership that is particularly appropriate in education. Most educators would consider their job a *calling* rather than simply a *profession*. Nearly all teachers have some story to tell about why they gravitated to teaching and what makes them stay despite the long hours and low pay. "Leading from the heart" reminds us to remain in touch with the emotional, and even spiritual, motivation behind the work we do. It helps us connect with those things that really matter to us. When leaders keep this in mind and approach the formation

Expert Advice

Make sure you're in agreement with your community about what's best for your program. Don't get caught up in unimportant details. You don't need to "teach the laptop"—not even keyboarding. Students will get it. This isn't about making miracles but about *providing access to student resources and tools*. So make sure the community is absolutely clear that when you're adding technology, it's a long-term investment in student learning. You *must* think about total cost of ownership. Make sure everyone understands this. Very rarely do schools talk about what the total return on investment is.

— Barbara Catenaci, Beaufort County School District, South Carolina.

of a planning committee from this perspective, they can lead more effectively and empathetically.

For instance, how many doers and dreamers do you have on your committee? A planning committee tasked with formulating a vision for technology use in your school needs both. Everyone has some measure of these different human qualities, but some are naturally more comfortable being dreamers or visionaries, while others are more comfortable being doers. Dreamers are people who think big creative thoughts and ideas; doers want to get right to work on the tasks. You may find it helpful to assign certain roles and responsibilities to the visionary types and other tasks to the doers.

Many schools and districts have found that including key members of their parent body, board of trustees, and board of education can help the planning and marketing of a 1-to-1 program. A number of schools have pointed specifically to this strategy as a successful way to get parents on board and improve communications with all stakeholders. Whether and how this will work for you will depend on the culture of your school or district.

It's important to keep in mind, however, that while you need enough planning committee members to represent all stake-holder groups, the committee must remain small enough to manage effectively. You'll most likely have to assign pieces of the planning work to smaller task forces. While these task forces will be made up mostly of committee members, you may also include others from your school or district. This can be a good way to keep your committee manageable while generating input from others on specific, finite issues.

Surveying What Other Schools and Districts Are Doing

The good news for anyone considering the implementation of a new laptop program is that many good models and programs are already in existence (several of which we surveyed in part 1). When the original Anytime, Anywhere group of schools started in 1996, there were no 1-to-1 models to follow. Fortunately, this group saw the wisdom of banding together and learning from one another, and the research and documentation they've generated in the past 10 years provides us with many useful lessons and other keys to success. Today, we don't have to reinvent the wheel on 1-to-1; however, we do have to customize it to fit our schools' particular needs and purposes.

Cautionary Tale

In South Dakota, Teachers Push Back on Governor's Laptop Proposal

Governor Mike Mounds of South Dakota is experiencing what can happen when teachers aren't included in the planning stages of a 1-to-1 initiative. Mounds has proposed instituting a multimillion-dollar laptop program, but educators have balked, saying they'd like the money to be spent on other programs and resisting the state's top-down approach to educational reform. Fueling their disapproval is the fact that Mounds' plan calls for school districts to contribute to the 1-to-1 program's funding. South Dakota could use a Bette Manchester (see chapter 3's section on Maine), an educator with a vision who knows how to bring together disparate stakeholders. They'd also benefit from a Bruce Montgomery (see chapter 3's section on Michigan), who has helped Michigan secure outside funding for its laptop program. As this book goes to press, the future of the South Dakota initiative is unclear (see www.eschoolnews.com/news/showStory.cfm?ArticleID=6056).

The references and resources section in the back of this book (appendix B) is a good starting point for learning what other schools are doing with laptops and which models might work for you. The Lausanne Collegiate Laptop Institute, held each year in July in Memphis, is another good place to meet and learn from educators who are moving forward with 1-to-1 programs. This conference has grown quickly from 50 attendees in its first year, 2003, to more than 250 in 2005. It features several keynote speakers, dozens of concurrent sessions, and a host of laptop and tablet vendors ready to discuss your plans and needs and develop a customized solution for you. To learn more about this institute, go to www.laptopinstitute.com.

Schools with 1-to-1 programs seem particularly eager to share their experiences and know-how, so keep an eye out for articles about ubiquitous computing in *Learning and Leading with Technology, Education Week, Technology and Learning,* and other professional development publications. ISTE has several active special interest groups, such as SIG-TC, that deal with 1-to-1 issues, and most states have their own consortium of educational technology professionals, such as NJECC (New Jersey Educational Computing Cooperative) in New Jersey. Your state may also have an agency dedicated specifically to professional development and technology. For example, New York has BOCES (Board of Cooperative Education Services) and Pennsylvania has IU (Intermediate Units).

Independent school associations such as CAIS (Connecticut Association of Independent Schools), VAIS (Virginia Association of Independent Schools), and NYSAIS (New York State Association of Independent Schools) hold regular educational technology conferences that can inform your planning. ISTE's annual National Educational Computing Conference (NECC), the largest ed tech conference in the country, has a laptop strand that can be very helpful. Similarly, the yearly conference held by edACCESS, while geared more toward the nuts and bolts of technology rather than classroom implementation, can provide you with valuable grassroots support and information.

Starting on the Same Page

Whenever a school or district sets out to enact a program with as many potential implications as 1-to-1 laptops, it's crucial that everyone start on the same page. Consequently, you'll find it very helpful to gather core reports and publications from your school and assemble them in a binder for everyone on your committee. This may include your existing technology plan, the school's mission statement, the results of recent state assessments and No Child Left Behind reports, demographic reports on your students and teachers, and similar publications. Before moving ahead, it's important to know where you are and where you've been.

Expert Advice

It's my opinion that schools spend way too much time on direct training of computer skills. Our model is messier in that some kids may seem to struggle at first because they don't have a firm tech base, but after a few months their confidence surges. Students build a lot more self-confidence when they have to figure things out themselves. So don't spend a lot of time on the laptop itself, because the focus should be on the learning. Be patient and allow the program to evolve naturally and slowly, so long as your school culture can survive that; some schools may demand immediate evidence of success. If you let your laptop program evolve over time, it will be much stronger as a result.

— Howard Levin,
The Urban School, San Francisco

Next, you'll want to begin documenting your school's plans to implement a 1-to-1 program. Keep accurate records of all your committee meetings, communiqués, minutes, drafts, statements, and so on. Make sure these reports are action-oriented. Too many organizations have foundered in the planning stages of a new program because action items aren't regularly identified and no one is held accountable for seeing them through. You've probably attended plenty of meetings like this, where everyone leaves feeling energized and enthusiastic but nothing ever seems to get done. Every plan, idea, and fact-finding mission should have a deadline or target date for completion, and an individual or group should always be assigned responsibility.

Good documentation accomplishes a number of things:

1. You want to make sure everyone present at your meetings, as well as those unable to attend, will be able to read and comment on the plans you're making and the solutions you're coming up with.

2. You want to keep a record of your committee's progress so that others can understand its function and direction.

3. You may want to go back to these early documents at a later date to evaluate the progress you've made and the changes that have taken place to your original plan.

One of your committee's first tasks should be the creation of a mission statement for your laptop program, and this document should be added to your binder. It should be as specific as possible about the aims of the program and should tie each element and target to concrete educational objectives. What exactly do you expect to improve on or enhance with the addition of laptops in terms of measurable results for teaching and learning? What have you seen or read about at other schools that you think can work in your school and district and can be accomplished through 1-to-1 computing?

A word about privacy: some schools keep these planning committee documents private, and some do not. This again needs to be a decision based on your organization's culture and ground rules. However, carefully consider whether or not THWADI (That's How We've Always Done It) is the operative reason for many of your plans and decisions. If it is, actively search for new voices and new ways of approaching this planning process. You want to bring people on board as early as possible, and giving them a chance to review and comment on the planning, as it happens, is often the best way to do that.

Expert Advice

Pay strict attention to change management. There are two fundamental aspects to this: the people involved and the logistics of changing your technology.

I understand why some schools try to go whole hog on 1-to-1 during the very first year, but there is no real advantage to doing so in the long run. Schools that proceed too quickly may lose faculty members and experience unanticipated network problems, because everything, and everyone, is affected. The reality is that it's next to impossible to help the entire faculty integrate laptops all at the same time. If, instead, you ease into the implementation, you can use the previous year's groups to help prepare the next year's. Ultimately, both curriculum integration and classroom management go much smoother if you phase laptops in over time. Schools that don't do this often have to fire people 2 to 3 years down the road, because they end up with personnel they don't need once everything's in place. In fact, you may want to consider hiring people on a contract basis for a few years to help with your implementation.

Finally, make sure your manufacturer or vendor is a good partner and that you're not in it all by yourself. Confirm that the vendor is going to be there for you for the long haul—this relationship has to last.

— Alex Inman, Whitfield School, St. Louis, Missouri

Key Elements to Consider When Planning a 1-to-1 Program

Here's a list of key things to consider when planning a laptop program. More information on many of these topics will follow in later chapters.

PLATFORM

Inevitably, one of your first and most important decisions will be choosing a platform for your 1-to-1 program. Your options include Windows-based laptops and tablet PCs (manufactured by Dell, IBM, HP, Toshiba, and others); Apple laptops (iBooks and PowerBooks); Linux-powered laptops; thin clients; and Palm OS or Pocket PC handheld computers. There are pros and cons to all of these platforms, and plenty of opinions about which are the best, safest, and most suitable for education.

Manufacturers will go to great lengths to convince you that they offer the best solution for the best price, so it's a good idea to prepare for this marketing onslaught. As you visit other schools with 1-to-1 programs, ask them why they chose the platform they did and whether they'd choose the same platform again. Consider your current hardware, network, and support infrastructure and look for solutions that will be easy to integrate into your existing systems. Also consider the "value-added" piece of the various platform options: will you receive a lot of support from your hardware vendor in terms of class-room setup, warranties, technical support, repairs, attractive pricing or leasing deals, and so forth?

If you're expecting parents to purchase the laptops, you'll want to make the proposal as attractive and complete as possible. This may take the form of a package deal, with the computer, case, insurance, technical support, and warranty all built in. Some schools have taken a tiered approach to this, offering different levels of support and coverage for different prices. More and more vendors are now offering package deals in which all the components of a "standard" 1-to-1 laptop program are included.

Laptop consulting companies that offer a soup-to-nuts menu have sprung up recently, and one of these may be just to your taste. However, it's good to keep a popular Internet acronym in mind here: YMMV (Your Mileage May Vary). Arm yourself with as much knowledge as possible before you start negotiating package deals and prices. Attend laptop conferences, visit other 1-to-1 schools, reach out to all the known hardware vendors (Apple, Dell, IBM, Hewlett-Packard, and so on), talk to your local technology consortiums, and keep up-to-date on the latest deals and offers.

As mentioned above, platform decisions should be considered in light of your existing network and support infrastructures. They should also be considered in light of existing human resources. If you have no one who understands Linux, for example, it's probably not a good idea to buy 200 Linux machines, even if they come at a really good price. If most of your computer technicians are Mac-illiterate, Windows-based laptops are probably your best option. But if you're a school with a long history of using Macintosh computers and have all those support pieces and relationships in place, iBooks make more sense.

Software resources should also be considered when deciding on a platform. Some vendors require platform-specific licenses. This means that even though you may already have 1,000 licenses for a particular product, those licenses may not be transferable to a different platform. Then, there's the issue of compatibility. Even though software has become much more compatible cross-platform than 10, or even 5, years ago, there can be user interface and translation problems when moving to a different operating system. Microsoft, for instance, is infamous for not always keeping products such as Office current with its most up-to-date Windows operating system. Apple has historically done a better job of this, but Internet bulletin boards are full of anguished posts from frustrated Mac users complaining about the messy transition from OS 9.x to OS X. Again, review what software resources you have and want to keep and build that into your decision making.

You also have existing computer users to consider. Will teachers, students, administrators, and staff need to start from scratch and learn a completely different operating system from the one they've grown used to? Changing horses midstream is always difficult, but it's particularly challenging when 24/7 technology integration is your goal. If you decide to switch platforms, be sure you have identified a really compelling set of reasons for the switch and be prepared to explain and defend those reasons with skeptical teachers and staff.

Most servers will support a variety of clients, but the complexity of network administration seems to increase exponentially when you have multiple client platforms. In my experience, most schools with both Macintosh and Windows computers usually have one dominant platform in terms of numbers of machines. Regardless of which platform is in the minority, that platform seems to eat up the lion's share of the network administrator's time simply because it's separate and different. Even though major hardware and software products have come a long way in terms of compatibility, there are still plenty of programs that inevitably seem to cause problems when you're trying to update your anti-virus software, install new administrative software, upgrade your network switches, or perform other network maintenance. Avoid that complexity if you can by sticking with your current dominant platform.

INFRASTRUCTURE

Do you have adequate cabling and electricity in place to support your laptop program? Once you've chosen your platform, and even if you choose to go wireless, you'll still need adequate Ethernet cabling in your walls or ceilings, because the wireless access points and networked printers have to connect to something.

You'll probably want network "drops" (connections) in many rooms as well, to connect back to your main file server. Network drops for shared printers will be necessary, as will surge-protected electrical outlets for a classroom full of laptops. Despite recent advances in battery technology, some laptops will struggle to make it through a full day of school, particularly if students are using CD or DVD drives or powering peripherals through their laptop. Think ahead about how student laptops can be recharged efficiently during the day. At Peck, we've found that as long as students make sure their iBooks get a full charge overnight (as they are required to do) and turn their machines off during the day when they're not using them, the laptops will make it through most, if not all, of the day. Students should continually monitor their battery indicator. Spare batteries, power adapters, and outlets should be made available as needed.

If you plan to go wireless, locating the wireless access points so as to ensure uninterrupted coverage is also a critical planning need. At Peck, we originally set up our wireless network about 5 years ago and thought we'd done a pretty good job, but we've had to make a lot of refinements in the years since. We'd already pulled Ethernet cable through the walls, so adding wireless capability entailed installing Apple AirPort devices on ceilings and walls near existing network drops and having our in-house electrician bring electricity to the devices.

Two new buildings are under construction at The Peck School, and they'll be outfitted with gigabit Ethernet cabling and newer network switches. Everything will be designed to work with the network hardware that we already have in place. For this work, we contracted with a local systems integrator that specializes in the design and installation of new networks that integrate with an existing network infrastructure.

This company has helped us determine the best location for switches and other network devices (with Ethernet this is mostly about distance—you can go about 300 feet from switch to switch without another device). The contractor has also advised us on the type and capacity of switches needed (leaving room for future growth), helped with cable installation, and provided us with a Windows server engineer who's made sure that everything will work on our existing servers. The company has also redesigned our server room, which will soon be moved to one of the new buildings. We've taken advantage of this new constriction to relocate the wireless access points for our entire campus, fixing interference problems and eliminating "dead spots."

Adding cabling or wiring to an existing building requires going back to the original network plan and hiring a firm to run new cable where needed. The thickness and material composition of the walls, the distance between switches, the location of electrical wires, and other factors must be considered. Data cables have certain requirements different from those of phone cables. For example, data cables must not be crimped, bent, or stapled. Early in my career I worked for an organization that hired telephone contractors to pull data cable, and they'd stapled and bent the cable so much it no longer worked. This shouldn't happen today, because any professional cabling contractor should understand and have experience with both data and phone cable. Still, schools should be sure to hire contractors familiar with data cabling who offer warranties on their work.

NETWORK

What is the state of your network? Will it be able to handle the addition of, say, 40 mobile computers? How about another 300 mobile computers? Things to consider here include:

NETWORK OPERATING SYSTEM. Will your network and the operating system of the new laptops coexist effectively? The Peck School, for example, has both Macintosh and Windows computers, but our servers are Windows-based. We made this decision because we needed to run administrative programs that require Windows servers. With active directory and Macintosh network services, it all works for the most part. We did have to address printing issues and install a print server so that both Windows and Macintosh computers could find all the printers on the network. But network downtime is rare and usually has more to do with hardware failure (such as a network card) rather than an operating system problem. Still, this is an issue we frequently revisit.

NETWORK BANDWIDTH. You may have enough Internet bandwidth through your existing service provider to serve your needs now, but what will happen when you add dozens of new computers to your local area network? This is particularly crucial if you hope to support the use of streaming media in the classroom. At Peck, we've previously used ISDN and DSL connections, and now we have a T1 line. As costs for high-speed Internet access continue to come down, we take advantage by purchasing a faster connection whenever possible.

INTERNET FILTERING. Since all schools that accept federal money are supposed to filter their Internet access, chances are you already have a filtering or proxy system in place. How will you add laptops to that system? Some all-in-one programs, such as Websense, may work for your program. At Peck, we use Symantec's SMTP gateway and their Enterprise Solution. For a yearly fee we purchase licenses for anti-virus protection and Web and e-mail filtering for every computer in the school.

Cautionary Tale

SPIM

Add SPIM to your list of jargon for the technology age. It refers to Instant Messaging SPAM that can infect your whole network when an IM user clicks on a message link.

NETWORK SECURITY. You'll need to block ports, set up firewalls, and consider what students may be able do and get to on your network. You'll have many different hardware, appliance, and software-based security solutions to choose from; you'll likely need to use multiple devices and approaches. You'll also need a good network manager to continually monitor and adjust your network settings.

WIRELESS CAPABILITY. Wireless networking is probably in your future if you don't already have it. Most new laptops sold today have wireless capabilities built in. Consider your networking options before making any big purchases: Is setting up a wireless network a possibility for your school or district? How many network access points will be necessary to ensure adequate coverage? Where would they be located? If you already have wireless access points in place, make sure they'll interface with the wireless devices on your laptops. Wireless networking comes with its own set of security considerations. At Peck, we set up passwords and hard code them on the laptops. We also discourage visitors from using our wireless network without permission.

ANTI-VIRUS, ANTI-SPAM, AND ANTI-SPYWARE SOFTWARE. Students will likely be taking their laptops outside the school network to their homes and other potentially unsecured locations. This increases the chances that viruses, Trojan horses, worms, spyware, and other nefarious programs may get onto their machines—and thence, onto *your* network. How will you scan these computers for viruses and protect your servers from infection from within? Be sure all your servers are continually updated and have the highest protection available. Also consider methods to scan every laptop on a daily basis.

Chapter 7 will offer further information on many of these items.

TECHNICAL SUPPORT

Schools often underestimate their needs for technical support. You'll almost certainly have to add personnel to support your laptop program, even if parents and students are purchasing their own laptops.

Technical support for laptops is different from desktop support for several reasons. Since laptops go back and forth from school to home, the risk of damage, loss, and malware infection is much higher. Some students and faculty will want to connect their laptops to their home networks as well as the school network, so the computers will have to be configured for both. For this reason, you should budget for at least one additional technical support person just for your laptop program.

As you add personnel, be sure they have the proper mix of people and technical skills. Supporting teachers and students should be their priority, not the hardware or network. In the words of education technology consultant Rick Bauer (personal communication, October 15, 2004), "Technical Support = Empathy + Competence." A healthy dose of both from your technical support staff will go a long way toward ensuring not only that your computers are up and running, but that your students and teachers feel supported and respected as well.

Expert Advice

Give teachers laptops long before they're issued to students. Develop a strong, stable infrastructure and hire a top-notch tech support staff. Separate network and non-instructional decisions from instructional decisions. Invest in staff development. Visit other schools. Don't let students buy the laptops; the school should own them! Have a strong RUP (Reasonable Use Policy) and enforce it for both staff and students. Treat technology as just another classroom tool. Its use should be seamless and transparent, not a gimmick or gadget.

— John Durham, Cannon School, Concord, North Carolina

FUNDING

We'll discuss funding options in more detail in chapter 7. There are as many ways to fund a laptop program as there are school districts and schools.

Depending on which platform you choose, whether you lease or buy, and the types of support you'll pay for, costs for 1-to-1 programs vary widely. What should be clear from the outset, however, is that funding a laptop program is not just a one-time capital expense. It requires continuous, yearly funding that's likely to increase year-to-year due to inflation and other factors.

To ensure the continuity and stability of your program, it's a good idea during the planning stages to identify precisely how your laptop program will be funded for a set period of years. Three or more is recommended.

PROFESSIONAL DEVELOPMENT

Carefully consider how you'll bring teachers on board and how you'll expose them to effective models for integrating laptops into their teaching. Making sure teachers feel comfortable using laptops is crucial to the success of your program. If teachers aren't familiar with the online resources and integration strategies that work best in their subject areas, and if they aren't continually adapting their teaching practices to fit a learning environment where every student has a networked laptop computer, your program won't thrive and move ahead. Chapter 6 will delve into these issues in greater detail.

COMMUNICATION

Have a plan for communicating with all stakeholders, even while your committee is still formulating plans, goals, and approaches. Communication problems are common in many organizations, and they often stem from a failure to articulate institutional changes and visions.

Sometimes schools hold onto information too closely while plans are still being made, feeling that it's not a good idea to broadcast half-formed ideas and invite criticism or ridicule. However, most experts say that frequent and timely communication is an important tool for change management and an indicator of the health of an organization. So don't be afraid to share what's going on even if your plan isn't completed. The professionals in your organization will appreciate it.

Encourage anyone with questions to come to members of the committee for answers, and budget time to answer these questions as they arise. Eliminating any perceived mystique or secretiveness in the planning process will help everyone buy into the program. Be respectful of those with differing opinions and let them have their say. They may be voicing worthwhile ideas and legitimate concerns that others on your committee haven't articulated but which need to be considered as you move ahead.

SUGGESTIONS FOR MANAGING CUSTOMER EXPECTATIONS

Adapted from the action plan in Naomi Karten's book, *Managing Expectations: Working with People Who Want More, Better, Faster, Sooner, NOW!*

1. Guard Against Conflicting Messages. Identify changes you can make so that your standards and your actions are in sync.

2. Use Jargon with Care. Initiate a review of your most widely distributed written material, and make changes to eliminate possible gaps in clarity or precision.

3. Identify Communication Preferences. Analyze your customers' preferences, and identify changes that will enable you to work more effectively with them.

4. Listen Persuasively. Analyze each other's listening style, and identify changes that might improve the impact you make on customers.

5. Help Customers Describe Their Needs. Identify ways in which you can give customers something to serve as a focal point for explaining their needs.

6. Become an Information-Gathering Skeptic. Create a master list of questions that can guide you in challenging your customers' assumptions and your own.

7. Understand Your Customers' Context. Prepare a list of information-gathering questions to help you broaden your perspective of your customers' problems.

8. Try the Solution On for Size. Identify methods you can use to help customers "try on" the solution earlier in the project cycle.

9. Clarify Customer Perceptions. Identify changes you can make that will help customers better understand how you can help them.

10. Set Uncertainty-Managing Service Standards. Evaluate the advantages and pitfalls of your group's approach to setting service standards.

11. When Appropriate, Just Say Whoa. Identify situations in which you might just say whoa, so customers don't expect more than you can reasonably deliver.

12. Build Win-Win Relationships. Formulate methods for strengthening relationships with your customers, including at least one you view as difficult.

IMPLEMENTATION

Implementation issues are also described in detail in chapter 7, but for now start thinking about your goals, requirements, and implementation date so that you can work backward from this target date when filling out your plan. Management experts talk about the "critical path" that all successful projects should take:

▶ identifying the individual tasks and requirements

▶ setting timelines and dates for each

▶ continually monitoring progress so that planners will know at once how each component may impact project completion

Using this technique will help your program stay on target. For instance, if a certain type of laptop case isn't available in the quantity you want for the first day of school, will this affect your critical path? What's Plan B? *Is* there a Plan B?

You should also keep your various constituencies in mind as you plan your program's implementation timeline: how will you bring your teachers, parents, taxpayers, board members, and the community at large fully on board? Planning informational evenings, press releases, and interviews with project leaders are measures other schools have taken to ensure that everyone affected by the program is properly informed.

ASSESSMENT

Schools often think they're done when laptops are finally handed out and the program officially begins. However, this isn't the time to disband your committee and congratulate members on a job well done. Instead, this is when managing change becomes most important. Your committee should continue to meet on an ongoing basis to address problems that occur and assess progress being made. You may at this point want to invite additional people, particularly from your teaching staff, to join the committee.

Once the hoopla is over, the press has moved on to other stories, and teachers start to integrate the laptops into their classrooms in small and large ways, the real learning begins. According to the anecdotal reports included in part 1, most laptop-using teachers and students say they do *not* want to go back to their pre-laptop days. But without steady stewardship and continual assessment, 1-to-1 laptop programs can start to morph and move away from your original educational goals, becoming nothing more than a program of electronic pencils.

Be sure, then, that there's a process in place to monitor the ways laptops are being used in the classroom. Make it clear to teachers that they're expected to use the laptops for meaningful learning, not merely for automating classroom routines. As will be detailed in the next chapter, regular and ongoing professional development is the most important component of this process.

Conclusion

We all know examples of educational initiatives that didn't work. Inadequate planning is nearly always a factor in these failures. If you can make your program planning a continual, reiterative process, your 1-to-1 laptop program stands a very good chance of becoming integral to your institution's overall educational mission.

Chapter 6
PROFESSIONAL DEVELOPMENT FOR TEACHERS

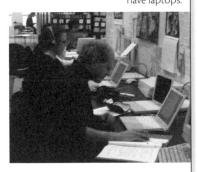

Introduction

TEACHERS ARE KEY to the success of any 1-to-1 program. While students will readily gravitate to their new laptops and use them willingly to download music, write reports, and organize their work, teachers are often a bit harder to get on board. If they aren't convinced of the value of technology in general, and of 1-to-1 laptops in particular, they'll be slow to make the changes in pedagogy and classroom management that take the greatest advantage of a 1-to-1 environment. Thus, many of the potential benefits of your investment in laptops will be lost. While students will still be able to do meaningful work with their laptops, their experience in the classroom won't change very much if teachers don't embrace the new technology.

If first-time visitors to a big city don't have a map, a plan, or a tour guide, they'll probably happen upon a few interesting things at random but will likely miss the local Louvre, the city's best restaurant, a fascinating historical site, and so on. Similarly, without some type of guidance from their teachers, students with laptops will find some things to interest them and occupy their time, but they'll probably not use them in the most educationally effective and transformative ways possible. To ensure that teachers can play the role of trusted "guide on the side," they need professional development that's relevant to the content area and age group they teach and that helps them consider how laptops can enhance and transform what they're doing in the classroom.

Professional Development—Vital to 1-to-1 Success

Nearly everyone agrees that professional development in technology integration is essential for teachers who want to learn how to adapt their instructional practices to the digital tools increasingly available to them. But finding the time and resources necessary to fund this vital training—which must be iterative, sustained, and understood by all parties to be an individual and institutional priority—has proved to be one of the key challenges of education technology integration. The need for timely and comprehensive professional development is only heightened in a 1-to-1 program. As Barrios writes, "Lack of targeted, sustained support for teachers in integrating technology with the curriculum has been identified as a major barrier to a successful one-to-one computing environment" (2004/ March 22, p. 16).

Teachers new to 1-to-1 must be provided with meaningful examples of laptop integration that relate specifically to their content areas. These models will help them recraft their lessons and projects to take advantage of ubiquitous access. They also need help with classroom management and technology management issues. 1-to-1 programs can thrive or disintegrate on this one issue alone, so it's absolutely crucial that program planners carefully consider how they'll provide teachers with technical support and training in integration.

Critical questions to consider include:

▶ How can you encourage teachers and administrators to buy into the need for continuous and intensive professional development in technology?

▶ When, how, and how often will this professional development occur?

▶ Who will lead these professional development sessions: the early adopters among your staff and faculty, outside consultants and trainers, or a combination of the two?

▶ Who will follow through and evaluate the effectiveness of this professional development, and who will assess how well teachers are transferring it to the classroom? How will you respond to teacher feedback and customize the training to particular needs and project interests?

▶ How much will this professional development cost, and how will you pay for it? Will faculty be compensated for the training, will substitute teachers need to be hired, and will salary increases and incentives be tied to its successful implementation in the classroom?

▶ How and when will follow-up and reach-out to teachers occur after training sessions?

Some 1-to-1 schools have used survey tools and other pre- and post-laptop assessments to track changes in teacher attitudes and student perspectives regarding technology use in the classroom. This can be very helpful in planning and monitoring professional development efforts. If you do this, be sure to continue the assessment for several years to avoid being overly influenced by the honeymoon effect that can occur when new technology is first introduced. Conversely, you don't want to overreact to the frustrations that may be caused by initial technical problems and program growing pains.

Professional development comes in many different forms, and not all forms are equally appropriate and useful for learning how to integrate technology. Some of the best ed tech workshops I've attended were the ones that gave partici-pants plenty of time to work in groups, laugh about common problems, and share stories from the classroom regarding integration successes and failures. At one such workshop, the leader had us working in groups of three or four to tackle student technology lessons, giving us a student's-eye view of what teachers were asking their students to do with tech-nology. This workshop opened many eyes.

Some of the worst workshops I've attended, on the other hand, were those where teachers were told to follow step-by-step, rote instructions. In fact, I myself have led workshops like this (before I knew better!), and while everyone left knowing something new, most later returned to me with many questions and a total lack of confidence in their own ability to explore and try new things with the technology. In other words, when I wasn't there to tell them which key to press, they felt lost and frustrated.

While linear, discrete instruction is often an important element of professional development workshops, teachers also need to be given time to reflect, work in groups, and share ideas and experiences. Remember to allow for some "Aha!" moments for your teachers, just as you would for your students.

Teacher Buy-In

Teaching is one of the most stressful of all professions. Turnover is high. Early burnout is common because teachers are, generally speaking, overworked, underpaid, and under-valued by our society. Teachers feel pressured from many sides: from students, parents, and administrators, as well as from state and national governments. Standards must be taught and adhered to, students are being tested like never before, and it all keeps coming back to the work of the class-room teacher.

Consequently, it's never a good idea to simply present teachers with a classroom full of laptops and a whole new set of expectations without first preparing them and soliciting their input. Teaching practices and classroom manage-ment strategies will (and must) change in a 1-to-1 environment, and teachers need to be supported throughout this transition.

It's crucial first of all to convince teachers of the value of teaching with laptops and demonstrate how this technology can help their students. Some ways to do this include:

▶ Give all your teachers laptops before you give them to students. Let them get familiar and comfortable with their digital assistant as a user before asking them to facilitate student use.

Lessons Learned

The Urban School's Approach to Professional Development

The Urban School leveraged the relationships between students and teachers with this innovative professional development program:

A key to building faculty skills and interest was offering summer technology workshops that were project-based. We offered a week of non-agenda-based tech support workshops. Teachers met with me before the workshops began and came into them with their own project plan. They chose something that would have immediate applicability in class. We hired student tutors and paired them with the teachers to help with the projects. We told the students not to touch the keyboard but to simply be a guide, and not do the work for the teachers. We did this for 3 years, and it was a great success.

— Howard Levin, The Urban School, San Francisco

▶ Train a cadre of tech-savvy students to support teachers. Be careful to set expectations appropriately: students should always be respectful of their teachers' needs and their level of technology expertise. Not all teachers will feel comfortable seeking technical support from students, particularly early on in the program. Allow teachers to opt out if this is a problem for them.

▶ Reach out to master teachers and early adopters of technology who have led previous innovations and seem open to exploring new approaches. At The Peck School, one of our math teachers immediately took to the use of the electronic whiteboard and communicated his enthusiasm to other teachers so energetically that it became contagious. This grassroots movement was all the more powerful because it was started by a fellow teacher who was not previously known as much of a techie. Encouraging this type of peer-to-peer sharing is an excellent way to inspire buy-in.

▶ Have your technology coordinator or facilitator schedule informal drop in sessions and post a welcoming sign on their door so that teachers know they can come in with even the simplest and most embarrassing of technical questions, such as, "How do I turn this on?"

▶ Hang out in the faculty room or near the copier or coffee-maker. Take your laptop there and be ready to talk to people who come in. Teachers often have limited time during the day to relax and unwind. Be approachable and available when teachers have a moment to think and reflect, but be sure not to make anyone feel cornered or on the spot.

▶ Publish and present your programs' successes frequently, and make this a teacher-led process, not technology-department-led.

Surveys are a good tool for gauging teacher attitudes and soliciting feedback in an unthreatening, anonymous way. Conduct a survey before, during, and after you start up your laptop program. If done thoughtfully, surveys can help you identify and address concerns quickly and track your success in real time. Surveys should be anonymous and include both discrete response and open-ended questions. Keep the length short and be honest about how much time it will take and how the results will be used.

Share ideas and strategies during meetings and other venues, but avoid putting too much paper in mailboxes and sending out too many e-mails. In the past, I've been too prolific in this regard, and it hasn't proved useful. Too much communication dilutes your message and elicits groans. Targeted information is best. If you know fourth-grade classes are studying Colonial America, for example, go ahead and send teachers resources and links that you know will be appropriate to what they're already doing in the classroom. Be sure to tell teachers why and how you think these resources can be

Expert Advice

Don't expect everything to work perfectly the first day. Every teacher is different, and it will take time to train them all. One year you're doing word processing, the next year electronic grade books. You're not going to come to the end of it. It's always going to be more expensive than you thought. Don't get frustrated. Find your ed tech colleagues and network and meet with them. Share. Commiserate. Pass around information.

Some schools see one another as competitors. Technical people don't seem to. Don't go it alone. Look around and communicate with others who are doing the same things you are.

— Elizabeth Cohen, St. Thomas, Coral Gables, Florida

valuable to them; don't ask them to click blindly through 20 URLs trying to figure out what's being offered on these sites.

On the other hand, don't err in the opposite direction and wait for teachers to come to you. General e-mails to all staff saying, "Come see me when you have time," will rarely be answered, since no one *ever* has enough time. Know your teachers, what they're teaching, and how they like to teach. If you have a curriculum map for each grade level, refer to it frequently and pay close attention to overarching themes and time frames. Going out to teachers with something specific and targeted to their curriculum, and timed so that they can use it right away, will really encourage them to see you as their ally. Remember that it's always easier to edit than create. Consider starting a document for a teacher with some preliminary information filled in—say, a student rubric for evaluating Web sites about China—and then ask the teacher if this would be useful in their classroom.

Respect the learning curve of adults. Not everyone learns, understands, and assimilates information in the same way and at the same speed. Make a point of saving all e-mail correspondence to and from your teachers. In my experience, teachers will often come back having remembered something you sent them months ago, ready to discuss it but unable to locate their copy.

Reach out to those you know aren't on board. Sometimes schools and districts hesitate to do this, but I've found a good deal of success with this approach. If particular individuals at a meeting are clearly uncomfortable with what's happening, seek them out later and see if you can get them to open up. You can't solve every problem, but you can negotiate and compromise and you'll get credit for simply hearing them out. Listen carefully to your teachers when they have questions or concerns, and attend equally to their words and body language. Don't interrupt, and don't talk until they seem ready to hear you. Repeat their messages back to them so that they know you've heard and understood.

Make sure your technical support staff is friendly, empathetic, nonjudgmental, and respectful of teachers' time and their level of technological expertise. Condescension is always easy to spot and can quickly destroy all your efforts at soliciting teacher buy-in. Leave out the jargon unless it's educational jargon that all teachers know and will respond to. Find ways to explain technical details without sounding technical.

Lessons Learned

Technology Fellows at Bancroft School

Noticing the proliferation of laptop programs for students and faculty in the area, Bancroft School in Worcester, Massachusetts, decided to test the waters with a group of committed faculty to see what laptops might bring to their own school. Administrators provided each of these "technology fellows" with a laptop, carrying case, and digital camera for a 2-year pilot program. The school also paid them a stipend of $250 to attend a weeklong professional development seminar. After 2 years, this cadre overwhelmingly recommended to the administration that the laptop program be expanded to all faculty members. Their reasons included:

- "Productivity and organization increases, and there's less paperwork."

- "Lessons can be prepared anywhere on a laptop."

- "I can pick up my desk anytime and go anywhere to work."

- "It's much easier to connect to LCD projectors, so I include them in my lessons more often."

- "Laptops are easy to access, reliable, flexible, and liberating!"

—William Brooks, Bancroft School, Worcester, Massachusetts

Finally, use mandates sparingly. While it's important that administrators make it clear that technology use is an expectation, avoid heavy-handed, top-down approaches. Teachers should be reminded of school or district mandates only as a last resort.

Working with Adult Learners

Teachers are adult learners, so it's important to know something about adult learning styles and what research tells us are effective strategies in teaching them. According to Malcolm Knowles (1984, p. 12), a leading theorist in the field of andragogy (adult learning), the essential characteristics of adult learners include the following:

► they are self-directed

► they want relevancy in what they are learning

► they want to know the goals of what they are learning

► they want to do, not just watch

► they want time to digest, think, and take a break

► they want to fit the learning into what they already know

► they have a wealth of knowledge

► they prefer to learn in ways that maximize their own learning style

► they want to learn cooperatively

► they want to have some involvement with the instruction and evaluation

While these aren't particularly new ideas, we still sometimes conduct technology workshops using the same industrial age instructional models we were subjected to as kids: putting everyone into heterogeneous groups across disciplines and grade levels, requiring everyone to follow a teacher-directed activity step-by-step, and providing little opportunity for peer sharing and discussion.

Leading effective workshops and professional development sessions takes careful thought and a constructivist, learner-centered approach. The best technology workshops:

► target the specific needs of the teachers participating

► give learners time to practice what's been taught and explore the tool for themselves

► put people in peer groups and allow them to do activities as a group

► fulfill a need that teachers recognize

► provide something intrinsically valuable that learners can use immediately

► include a "what did you learn and what will you do with it?" debriefing time

► have both an assessment and a follow-up component

► are fun!

Expert Advice

Take a semester to set goals. The next semester have everyone integrate two activities or projects. The first shouldn't be that big, nor should the second. Expect some degree of failure; if these first projects are anything other than a massive disaster, you've done a great job. Then, evaluate the process, and have teachers think about what worked, what didn't, and how to do it better the next time.

— Alex Inman, Whitfield School, St. Louis, Missouri

Another familiar concept—the idea of "learning communities"—can be a useful principle in designing professional development programs that effectively serve the needs of adult learners. You can foster the development of learning communities in many ways, particularly given the communication and technology tools now available.

E-mail, the Internet, blogs, wikis, instant messaging, listservs, Moodle, Blackboard, and a host of other free and fee services represent ways teachers can be encouraged to reach out to other educators and learn from their peers. Some ideas for using these technologies to promote learning communities include:

E-MAIL. E-mail can be used to facilitate asynchronous communication and sharing. You can use it both within your institution and with colleagues around the world. Some e-mail systems, such as FirstClass, offer group mailboxes that work like virtual conferences. When individuals send an e-mail to a group mailbox, the message is available for everyone to read and respond to. For example, at The Peck School, students have a highly successful conference called Student Council. Everything from salad dressing to sports to the homecoming dance is open for discussion. This forum gives all of our students a voice, a sense of community, and some say in how things are done at the school.

BLOGS. Blogs, a word derived from "Web logs," are open, online journals or bulletin boards that allow anyone interested in a particular topic to post ideas and opinions and respond to other people's postings. Blogs have exploded in popularity in the past year or two. There are now literally millions of them, covering every conceivable topic. Meta-blogs such as Technorati continuously monitor the "blogosphere"; to see an example of recent postings on the topic of 1-to-1, go to www.technorati.com/tags/1to1/.

WIKIS. Wikis are user-generated, collectively authored databases of information that take particular advantage of the hyperlinked nature of the World Wide Web. All wiki entries are open and editable by any user. The most famous wiki, Wikipedia (www.wikipedia.org), is an online encyclopedia that accepts contributions and clarifications from anyone. While there's some controversy over wikis' susceptibility to anonymous "vandalism" as well as questions about the accuracy of the information gathered in them, wikis' very openness is their best security measure, since chances are high that inaccurate, biased, or inflammatory postings will be quickly identified and edited.

INSTANT MESSAGING (IM). Instant Messaging is a synchronous communication technology that has quickly become wildly popular with students—but not so popular with teachers. While legitimate security and classroom management concerns related to IM have led many schools to outlaw its use in the classroom, I believe IM is the wave of the future and will be gradually embraced by teachers and administrators because of its value as an interactive authoring and collaboration tool.

Expert Advice

Skills are more readily internalized when professional development for educators takes place both *in context* and in *learning communities*. Technology skills taught in the context of a specific project and combined with teachers working communally—discussing, learning together, testing different possibilities—can be a catalyst for generating new ways to use computers in the classroom.

— Dr. Donna DeGennaro, Montclair University, Montclair, New Jersey

MOODLE, NICENET (both free), AND BLACKBOARD (fee-based). These classroom management tools are being used by schools and districts to organize and publish curricular materials, schedules, assignments, assessments, and student performance data. They're also used to create a forum for online discussions. In the New York City area, the NYCIST forum for independent school technology administrators and staff uses Moodle to set up online courses taught by members for members.

Professional Development Approaches—Varied, Frequent, Not Boring!

To be successful, professional development needs to be varied, iterative, and fun. There should be opportunities to share, take part in hands-on individual and group activities, and receive training that provides information and skills immediately usable in the classroom. Some typical professional development structures include the following:

BOOT CAMP

Some schools and districts use the term "boot camp" to describe a summertime workshop that immerses teachers in technology for several days or a week at a time. Content and focus will vary, but teachers are actively encouraged to pull together and learn from one another as they tackle a number of different technology projects and models.

To keep teachers energized throughout the process, the best boot camp workshops will set aside ample time, equipment, support, downtime, and refreshments. This type of workshop often gets strong, positive reviews. If this approach seems right for your school or district, consider the following:

▶ provide incentives or stipends for all participants

▶ survey teachers beforehand so that you can target areas teachers need the most help with

▶ ask teachers to bring a lesson plan they are already using and help them integrate technology into that plan

▶ provide adequate staff for coaching, facilitating, mentoring, and technical support

▶ schedule downtime for relaxing and talking with peers

▶ make the training fun by using team T-shirts, hats, entertainment, decorations— whatever will work for your school or district

▶ create a theme for the week

▶ make each "day" shorter than a normal school day, and stick to your timing

INFORMAL DROP-IN SESSIONS

This can take the form of short, 20-minute "make and take" lessons for your teachers. These sessions can take place when schedules are more flexible, such as before or after school (as allowed by your school or district). They should offer training in discrete tools or techniques manifestly useful to teachers, such as creating rubrics, using e-mail to increase productivity, and downloading images from digital cameras.

Ideas to consider include:

▶ setting the stage for a "tech café" atmosphere—drop in, relax, learn something, no pressure!

▶ making sure enough people and materials are available to help everyone. If necessary, prepare an interactive version of lessons that can be handed out and completed on a computer by the teachers themselves.

SHOWCASE SESSIONS—"BAGELS AND BYTES"

Before or after school, arrange drop in sessions in selected teachers' classrooms to showcase particularly successful examples of technology integration. Prepare a handout that summarizes the salient features of a particular lesson or project, identifying the curricular and technology goals realized and offering a rubric or assessment piece as well.

You may want to videotape and edit parts of these projects and run these videos in a continuous loop while teachers address their colleagues. Alternatively, you may simply want a teacher to talk, show what was done, explain why it was valid, and relate what was gained from it.

Think carefully about how these projects might work for different subjects, disciplines, and grade levels, and be sure to share your ideas with teachers. These sessions should be short and open to all, and the bagels should be fresh—*not* soggy!

TEACHER KIOSKS

Clearly, there is a theme running through these various approaches: *teachers mentoring and learning from one another*. In a kiosk situation, teacher-presenters set up mini-workshops and poster sessions, allowing colleagues to walk around and browse for ideas.

Encourage your teacher presenters to

▶ provide information for how a particular project might apply to different grade levels and disciplines;

▶ prepare handouts, videotapes, and attractive displays;

▶ make sure there is adequate tech support before, during, and after the presentations.

Conclusion

There's no greater indicator of the success of your laptop program than teacher buy-in. Invest the necessary time, money, resources, and energy into making your teachers comfortable with the technology, and all of your classrooms will reap the benefits. Start with what your teachers need help with the most—the administrative and instructional work they do every day.

Important points to remember:

▶ Make sure professional development for teachers is relevant to the content area and age group they teach.

- ▶ Structure professional development in ways that respect and reward your teachers' time.

- ▶ Build in enough time for everyone to unwind, interact, and reflect.

- ▶ Provide a venue for learning communities to flourish. Teaching can be isolating and professional development should help teachers connect with one another.

- ▶ Give *everyone* something to take away and use immediately, either in the classroom or for personal productivity. Remember that your teachers are likely to be on many different levels in terms of fluency and comfort with technology, not to mention their differences in instructional philosophies, subject areas, grade levels taught, and so forth.

- ▶ Avoid giving teachers either too much or too little to do during workshops, and have a backup plan in case things don't work or people are bored or stymied.

- ▶ Vary instruction techniques and formats, and encourage *everyone* to have fun!

Chapter 7

IMPLEMENTATION AND LOGISTICS

Introduction

LAPTOP PROGRAMS ARE COMPLICATED VENTURES, with a whole host of logistical issues to plan for and resolve. Just the idea of having hundreds of portable computers roaming around campus, wirelessly accessing your network files and sharing resources, is enough to strike fear in the hearts of even the most resolute and confident of network administrators.

And if that isn't enough, these digital assistants will also roam *off* campus and be used in students' and teachers' homes, where network access protocols and security schemes may be entirely different. Then, they'll be brought back to campus, potentially carrying a whole menagerie of computer viruses, worms, Trojan horses, and adware eager to get onto your network servers. For network administrators, this sounds like the perfect formula for a full-fledged nightmare!

Figure 7.1
Students work together at Suffield Academy, unencumbered by wires.

Damage, loss, and theft are also concerns. When school computers remained in a supervised lab and were used only for teacher-directed activities, screens didn't break when poked by a pencil, and computers weren't dropped, stepped on, run over, or used as a shield in a snowball fight. In those days, additional insurance wasn't needed for individual computers, since they were included in the blanket policy that covered all school facilities.

This chapter will introduce you to some of the most important logistical challenges that typically come with a 1-to-1 laptop program. Once again, a number of great ideas are offered by educators working in the trenches who have faced and overcome these same logistical challenges.

Preparing Your School Network for 1-to-1

Since nearly 100% of schools and districts across the country have Internet access today (U.S. Department of Education, 2004), it follows that most of you reading this book will already have a computer network in your school or district. However, if you're in the early stages of planning a 1-to-1 laptop program, you may not yet have specific policies and procedures in place to cover computers that go back and forth between school and home networks.

As so graphically illustrated above, adding a laptop program will *greatly* increase the complexity of managing your network. It will probably require adding technical staff, and it will definitely add to the workload of your technology department. Planning for these logistical challenges is crucial to the long-term success of your program.

Expert Advice

Our small network simply wasn't ready for laptops. We did fine the first year, when we had merely a handful. But when we rolled out 300 laptops in the second year, the network fell apart—viruses, wireless problems, printer problems, you name it. Our unreliable network caused the faculty a great deal of frustration that year, but we've made tremendous progress since then.

— Karen Douse, Harpeth Hall School, Nashville, Tennessee

Just as you need a technology director to lead technology integration efforts throughout your school or district, you also need someone to manage, update, adapt, secure, and run your network. This network manager should be certified in a number of operating systems and networks, and will need regular professional development opportunities, including workshops and certification training. You may already have a good network manager in place, but it may be necessary to hire additional network administrators to handle the new services and security challenges that come with a 1-to-1 program.

The following are some basic computer network issues to consider when planning for 1-to-1.

FIREWALL

By now, most schools are using some sort of firewall to block ports and secure their network from unauthorized access or use. However, 1-to-1 will put added strain on your entire network, so it's best to review your current firewall to be sure it's up to the task.

For instance, if you don't want students to be able to use instant messaging during the school day, have you blocked all of the ports associated with IM? IM can "jump ports," so you may need to consider multiple measures, such as a firewall appliance, software solutions, or locking down workstations. Some of the most popular firewall appliances used by schools include Packeteer, Barracuda, and SonicWall. All of these products have their pros and cons, and they may or may not be compatible with your network architecture, so do your homework and choose carefully. As always, your most valuable asset will be a well-informed network manager who keeps up with security trends and emerging threats.

Do you have, or plan to have, Voice over Internet Protocol (VoIP) running on your network? If so, be aware that a variety of new threats are specific to this technology, and your firewall needs to be robust enough to handle them. Be sure that the company you choose to install your VoIP products will provide you with specific security advice and protection so that outside IP-specific attacks cannot get through.

VIRUS PROTECTION

Do you run an anti-virus program automatically on all of your computers? How are program and virus definition updates managed? While it's fairly easy to administer a virus protection program for all school-based workstations, it's more difficult to make sure student laptops that log on and off the network at odd times during the day are similarly protected and updated. At Peck, we have our anti-virus software set to automatically update during the day, and generally this doesn't intrude on schoolwork

The timing and management of anti-virus updates are important issues to consider. You'll need to determine what level of inconvenience users are willing to tolerate. You may be forced to make some tough decisions here, balancing the need to limit disruptions and downtime with the need to protect your data and network resources.

OTHER NETWORK SECURITY ISSUES

How have you balanced the security needs of your network with the needs of your students and faculty to use their computers as fully as possible? If, for example, you want to control students' ability to install programs on their laptops and stop certain system functions, can students still go home and use their laptops with their home Internet connections? If you're giving students 24/7 access but drastically limiting their ability to research through the Internet and download files, are you crippling the laptops' usefulness?

Cautionary Tale

The Kutztown 13: Monitoring Gone Awry

In Kutztown, Pennsylvania, lax network security measures at the local high school resulted in students' exploiting the very technology that administrators had set up to monitor student computer use to monitor the *administration's* computer use instead. The technology staff had not only chosen an easy-to-guess password for the administrator's account, but they had also taped it to some administrators' computers. Several students—being the natural explorers that we know they are—found and shared it. You can read about what happened next by going to www.wired.com/news/technology/0,1282,68480,00.html.

The moral of the story is: guard your administrative accounts, change the password frequently, and monitor your monitoring software as much as you can.

There are certainly different schools of thought on this. Several of the schools interviewed for this book "lock down" their student laptops, preventing students from changing any configurations or adding software. At The Peck School, we originally went this route, too, but we found it too cumbersome and limiting, especially since we wanted to encourage students to use their laptops at home. While we do risk students making problematic changes to their computers, it's a fairly simple matter to reimage the computers as needed and start all over.

Are security configurations regularly checked to make sure they're set and working the way you want them to? Many security products default to a security level that's either too high or too low. Tweaking these levels to respond to user needs and complaints will often be necessary, and this should be done several times a year.

Do you run a remote desktop product to check on network activity and computer use? We do this at Peck, and it's been quite useful as a monitoring tool. For instance, when students are working in groups, teachers will use the remote desktop utility to check their students' screens to be sure they haven't wandered away from the subject at hand. Other schools use ARD (Apple Remote Desktop) and similar products to both monitor appropriate use and check on student progress on assignments and projects. This unobtrusive approach to offering formative feedback and advice precisely when it's needed works especially well with adolescents, who often want to save face and not ask for help in front of their peers.

Expert Advice

Managing a laptop program is a huge logistical task. One major area of concern is the stress that laptops put on the networking infrastructure. We had to add a packet shaper and e-mail spam filter. While we might have purchased these even without a laptop program, they became essential when we got our laptops.

— Fred Bartels, Rye Country Day School, Rye, New York

E-MAIL

Do you have an SMTP gateway that scans your e-mail for viruses and spam? Have you set it up to filter both incoming and outgoing mail? We typically think of security threats coming from the outside, but if any of your laptop users has "caught" a worm or Trojan horse, he or she may unknowingly be sending out viruses or worms to others.

Does your Internet Service Provider (ISP) offer any anti-spam or anti-virus protection? This seems to be a growing trend and can provide another layer of security. At The Peck School, we have two levels of security: a Symantec SMTP gateway and Trend Micro's security products running on our ISP's T1 connection.

Is your e-mail set up to allow downloading and uploading of attachments? Provided your other security components are in place, this is usually safe and is an excellent way to get around defective floppy disks and CD-ROMs that aren't readable. Students can simply attach files to e-mails and send them to themselves or their teachers, going back and forth from home as needed. You may have to establish size limits on attached files and also block the uploading of certain types of files, particularly executables. There will be a fine balance required here, however: too many limits will make it difficult for users to get their work done efficiently.

INTERNET PROXY SERVERS AND FILTERS

Do you use a proxy server? Your laptops will most likely connect to the school network through a proxy server. You'll probably need settings for both home and school. At Peck, we've set up Home and School Internet connections on our iBooks. Macintosh's Safari is smart enough to know the difference and provide the proxy settings at school and not use those settings at home when Home is checked. Our network manager and technical support specialist make sure the settings are created and then adjusted over the summer so that the laptops will work seamlessly once the students get them in the fall.

Do you filter your Internet access? This is a federal requirement, so most districts do. How often is your filter updated? Do you also log everyone's Internet use? At Peck, we use Symantec's Enterprise solution, which includes an SMTP gateway for all e-mail traffic and Web content filtering. Since we're a K–8 school, we believe our students need this kind of protection. I've also used Websense to filter Internet content. Both products are easy to configure and update and allow users to prevent or allow specific Web addresses as needed. This means that if a teacher wants to use a particular Web site that for some reason is filtered out by one of our categories, we can add that site to our "safe" list. Many similar filtering products are available on the market.

PASSWORDS AND PRIVACY ISSUES

How are you keeping your data secure internally? This means making sure no one can see anyone else's files. Password protection and user grouping are two ways to protect data. At Peck, we assign teachers and administrators to groups and then allow those groups to get "rights" to certain files on the network. Users can see their own personal files, but they can only see other people's files when they've been given permission to do so.

How often are passwords changed? Do you allow short or long passwords? Can people reuse old passwords? Are letter and number combination passwords required? At Peck, passwords for e-mail, the network, and Internet access are all in effect. Since we're multiplatform (our laptops are Macintosh, while most of our servers are Windows), we haven't implemented, and prefer not to use, a one-password approach. This means users have to remember and input multiple passwords.

Some schools and districts have used LDAP (Lightweight Directory Access Protocol) to simplify access to all servers, but Peck hasn't done this and has no LDAP-accessible applications. With an LDAP solution, users logging onto your network need just one password, instead of several, to gain access to all services. When applications are LDAP-compatible, they share the password. It's like having a master key for all the doors in the building. Without this solution, students and teachers must input separate passwords for different resources: a password for the network, a password for the Internet, a password for e-mail, and so on.

Have you addressed FERPA (Family Educational Rights and Privacy Act) with regard to your network and electronic data? Check out the following site to learn the FERPA guidelines you need to consider: www.ed.gov/policy/gen/guid/fpco/ferpa/index.html. In general, FERPA guidelines require schools to make sure that only teachers and administrators who need to access student data can do so. Student records are password-protected and locked away from inadvertent viewing. You may have to check the access rights of your network groups to make sure they are in compliance with FERPA.

NETWORK STORAGE

How much storage space per user is allowed on the network? If you allow too much, you may find the temptation to save inappropriate files too great for some.

Our approach at The Peck School is to start everyone off with 100 megabytes and add more storage based on requests. When teachers and students are working on videos, we have in the past given them more. Lately, however, we've decided it makes more sense to have users save video files to their own hard drives and then burn them to DVD or compress them with QuickTime and save on a CD. It's an issue we continue to grapple with, and most likely we'll have to go to larger storage options in the future. iMovies have really taken off as an educational vehicle, and that means you'll need more storage for these big files.

FILE BACKUP

Is everything on your network backed up regularly? While you don't need a daily backup of every single file, you do need your entire network backed up on a regular schedule. If applications and databases aren't regularly backed up, a reinstall in the event of a server crash will mean a reconfiguration of all of them. This will require you to restore all program updates and possibly many months of records and changes (if these records and changes are even recoverable).

Have you tested your restore lately? Even if you back up regularly, you need to test the restore of these files to make sure your backup is running reliably and the restore feature works. You'll have to consider your network and bandwidth here. Peck's solution is to make sure everyone backs up files to the network. We don't back up on the fly or during the day when wireless files are going back and forth. We back up about 2 a.m. when no one is on the network and there's no wireless activity.

BLOCKING FILE TYPES AND FILE SHARING

Do you block certain file types—such as MP3s and other media and game files—from being freely passed around your network? This is a big issue and deserves careful consideration. At Peck, we do allow students to download legally purchased music to their computers. However, if any of their music, or any other files they may have downloaded, causes the computer to crash, only the normal applications will be reinstalled when the computer is reformatted. It's a fine line. We want our students to "own" their computers, but we also want them to understand that the primary use of their laptops should be school-related.

Expert Advice

Equipment issues are the flip side of having a good 1-to-1 laptop program. The equipment itself doesn't hinder the program, but viruses, spyware, and other nuisances do. Rather than spending 60% of my time on curriculum and 40% performing triage on equipment, I've found that this ratio has flipped since we brought the laptops online.

— Sandy Kennedy, Berkeley Preparatory School, Tampa, Florida

Do you block the sharing of hard drives on your network? If you allow this sharing, or simply don't monitor it, you may find students setting up their own peer-to-peer file sharing system to pass music files back and forth. You should block or turn off this feature unless there's a compelling educational reason to have it available.

PROGRAM UPDATES

Are all your mission-critical software products regularly updated? Is a log kept of this information? Are there special authentication issues related to laptops used in more than one network environment? There should be a regular update log and approach that can be accessed and viewed by your technology department, and more than one person should be trained on how to do these updates.

TECH SUPPORT AND MAINTENANCE

What's your priority—your network or your laptop users—as far as support and maintenance is concerned? The answer may seem obvious, but there will be times when you have to make this difficult call.

For example, what if a critical network update becomes available during the middle of the school day: do you shut down the network right away to install it, or do you wait until most users have logged off and left the school building? At the schools where I've worked, we've almost always chosen the needs of computer users over the network. It's important that your teachers know they're your priority even when you have to make a call now and then in favor of the network. You want technology to support the learning, not keep the learning from happening just to save time.

Other Considerations

Preparing your network for the addition of dozens, or even hundreds, of new and mobile users is job No. 1 for a new laptop program. Many other considerations, however, will be just as important to your program's start-up. Here are several of the most important:

PROTECTIVE CASES

You'll have to determine how best to protect your laptops when they're carried around at school and transported to and from home. Protective cases are crucial for safeguarding your big investment in laptops.

Many schools have opted for an "always-on" solution, which is a protective case that's attached to the laptop body and surrounds it at all times. This type of case is custom-fit to a particular laptop model and is generally not transferable to other models. Many schools have had success with these cases, even though some have reported that students occasionally do take the cases off. An always-on case will work best if it allows students access to all the ports and connections they typically need. Transportation to and from school with this type of case requires a backpack, ideally one with extra padding.

Another solution is a hard-sided case. This is what The Peck School has used. We originally negotiated a volume price for an expensive hard-sided case and asked parents to purchase it, through us, on the day we distributed laptops. We later found a similar hard-sided case for much less money and worked with a local luggage store to customize it with foam cut to the size of our iBooks. This has worked well as long as students put only the laptop, nothing else, in the case and leave it in the case as much as possible. However, we may consider going to the always-on case in the future.

STORAGE

There will be times during the day when laptops aren't in use—lunchtime, sports, after-school programs, and so forth. Consequently, you need to consider where the laptops can be safely and securely stored when they're not needed.

At The Peck School, we were able to retrofit cubbies to the building that houses our seventh- and eighth-grade classrooms. Cables and locks were affixed to these cubbies, allowing students to thread the cables through the case

Expert Advice

We use always-on cases. Our insurance claims dropped 60% when we switched to them. The biggest challenge is trying to get users to keep them in their cases. When they're pulled out, it puts a lot of stress and torque on the system board and other parts of the computer, and the system board welding comes loose.

— Alex Inman, Whitfield School, St. Louis, Missouri

Expert Advice

Require your students' families to pay the insurance deductibles. Buy a plan with a $100 deductible, and charge families $100 for first-time damage. Tell them it will be $150 for the second time and $300 for the third, because it is insurance, not a warranty. Only the chronically irresponsible will feel the pinch.

This tiered approach has worked for us. After we switched to this policy, the number of second-time claims dropped from about 30 a year to 10 or 12.

— Alex Inman, Whitfield School, St. Louis, Missouri

handles and lock the laptops to the cubbies for secure storage.

A certain amount of policing is still necessary, however, to make sure laptops are securely locked in place and not left around the school. At Peck, teachers who see an unsecured or unattended laptop will "kidnap" it and bring it to the division or technology head. The student will then have to retrieve it and face the consequences.

WARRANTIES AND INSURANCE

When purchasing laptops, ask for an extended warranty. This will cover normal wear and tear on your computers. Of course, not all laptop mishaps will be covered by a warranty: soda spills, animal interference, failed stress-testing experiments, and accidental drops, to name just a few. This is where insurance—either purchased by the school or paid for by individual parents—can make a big difference.

Some schools self-insure their laptop program, combining school funds and parent contributions and setting this money aside to pay for repair and replacement not covered by the manufacturer's warranty.

THEFT DETERRENCE

Schools can purchase identifying tags and permanently glue them to laptops to help recover lost or stolen computers. Each tag includes an identifying number as well as the toll-free telephone number of the company providing the tag. Anyone finding a lost or stolen computer can call the company, which then notifies the school or district.

Registering the IP or MAC addresses of computers while they're logged onto the network has been helpful for some large school districts and schools that have experienced internal theft. This allows the network manager to scan for the IP or MAC address of the lost or stolen computer and track its use. To work, however, this deterrence solution requires a managed network as well as managed switches so that the precise location of all laptops logged onto the network can be determined.

INSTANT MESSAGING

Imho im=nbt (In my humble opinion, instant messaging is the next big thing.)

Instant messaging, along with text messaging, has become *the* communication medium of choice for the millennial generation. Up to now, most schools and districts have limited IM, or outlawed it altogether, since it *can* be highly intrusive in a traditional classroom. However, it may prove to be the best way we can reach millennials and encourage their thoughtful collaboration if we, as educators, can figure out how to use this tool judiciously. A few schools have already begun experimenting with it as a way to offer students on-the-spot technical support and engage them in group conversations on school-appropriate topics.

Instant messaging offers its users a significant degree of anonymity. This disconnect from normal social interaction can be both a boon and a danger. Young people report that it's easier to say difficult or personal things via IM than to say them in person. That's one of the reasons students will often say things online they don't mean or wouldn't say in person. Sometimes these messages are vulgar, threatening, or sexually explicit. Thirteen-year-old boys have said that it's easier to IM a girl they like than talk to her in person. Sixteen-year-old girls have said they prefer to break up with a boyfriend using IM.

Is this avoidance of difficult situations and real world communication healthy? What are the long-term effects on students' communication skills and emotional development? We don't know the answers to these questions yet.

At The Peck School, we block IM and will continue to do so until we can identify a valid educational project that requires it. Even then, we'll probably turn it on only for that project. IM is a double-edged sword: the reactive and disruptive nature of this style of communication, along with its potential to be used for cheating, must be carefully considered and planned for if it's to find a place in most school settings.

Summer Preparation for Laptop Rollout

The following is a description of what we do at Peck School at the end of every school year and in the summer to prepare for laptop rollout in the fall:

APRIL–MAY

- ▶ Order computers as needed in time for summer delivery (Peck is on a 4-year replacement cycle for laptop computers).

- ▶ Negotiate deals and add-on features.

- ▶ Purchase extended warranties for all laptops.

- ▶ Interview and hire part-time summer tech staff.

JUNE

- ▶ Retrieve laptops from seventh- and eighth-grade students.

- ▶ Check inventory of hard-sided cases and order new cases as needed.

- ▶ Order theft deterrent plates.

- ▶ Assess the condition of eighth-graders' laptops to determine if repair or replacement bills need to be sent to parents.

- ▶ Order spare batteries and power cords as needed (we keep spares as loaners for students).

- ▶ Schedule faculty laptops for reimaging and updating (we're more flexible with faculty laptops, since teachers continue to use their computers over the summer to plan and develop curriculum; we also have many teachers who take summer workshops and seminars and need their laptops).

JULY–AUGUST

▸ Reimage all laptops, updating and reinstalling software as needed, checking for damage, and cleaning and repairing (some are repaired in-house, others are sent out).

▸ Image new computers, affix theft deterrent plates, and input serial numbers and information into hardware inventory database.

▸ Assign laptops to new and returning students. This process includes

  • database assignment by serial number and internal number;

  • updating and printing database forms, including the laptop assessment sheet to be signed by student and parent (see appendix A);

  • printing out labels with student name, laptop number, and name and address of the school, and inserting them into self-adhesive "luggage tags" affixed to the computer case;

  • determining cubby assignments (cubby number and lock combination are stored in the inventory database as well as typed into our student information database).

▸ Prepare laptop pickup packages for students, including laptop, power cable, Ethernet cable, locker, locker cable, and luggage tag.

▸ Set up network, Internet, and e-mail accounts and IDs for all students and faculty.

▸ E-mail and call all seventh-and eighth-grade parents to explain laptop rollout. Parents and students are responsible for

  • purchasing a laptop case,

  • reading and agreeing to the school's laptop policies and procedures (which includes sharing the costs for repairs not covered by warranty),

  • participating in an orientation session,

  • signing an inventory and assessment sheet which describes the condition of the computer (see appendix A).

Monitoring and Maintaining Laptops throughout the Year

Once laptops are in the hands of students and teachers, program administrators need to actively monitor usage and act quickly to fix problems as they arise so that curricular plans and schedules aren't disrupted by technical difficulties. Here are some of the most important things we do at Peck to ensure that laptops are being appropriately and effectively used:

▸ We regularly remind students about the appropriate care of laptops and the ethical use of all school computer equipment and resources. Peck uses the kid-friendly acronym LARK to help students remember that all use of school hardware, software, e-mail accounts, and Internet access needs to be:

L (Legal)—Only software and music that's been purchased can be downloaded; sources can only be used if they're cited and used appropriately.

A (Appropriate)—Everything viewed, sent, downloaded, and used on school laptops must be school-appropriate, not just to seventh- and eighth-grade students but to kindergarten students and grandparents as well.

R (Responsible)—Equipment and resources must be used carefully and responsibly to avoid the damage that results from neglect and poor handling.

K (Kind)—All e-mails and other electronic communications must be respectful and considerate of all parties; sending chain mail or any type of offensive or insulting material to anyone, is never kind.

▶ We review and redistribute our Acceptable Use Policy (see appendix A) several times per year and make sure students understand and adhere to it.

▶ Peck has found that a proactive approach to damage control and hard disk maintenance can be very helpful. While our Acceptable Use Policy and Laptop Guidelines (see appendix A) state that students should bring any damage or problems immediately to our attention, this doesn't always happen. Collecting computers several times per year allows us to assess computers for wear and tear, repair and correct problems, and update our assessment sheet.

Lessons Learned

Keep Track of Your Spare Parts

Keep a variety of spare parts on hand to minimize disruptions. Identify them by engraving an assigned number on every item, and log them in and out. At Peck, we used to hand out chargers without assigned numbers, and we discovered that students were freely borrowing chargers from one another and returning someone else's instead of their own. It turned into a huge problem. Students now have to return the specific charger they were assigned.

Implementation Challenges—The Experts Speak

Here are some first-person accounts of implementation challenges faced by other 1-to-1 programs.

SUFFIELD ACADEMY (SUFFIELD, CONNECTICUT)

Dean Ellerton, director of technology at Suffield Academy, lists these as the key challenges that his school has faced with their laptop program:

REPAIR "UPTIME." The more you rely on laptops, the more "downtime" is not tolerated. We've had to beef up staff (both adult and student technicians) to look at broken laptops in a timely fashion, and we've had to maintain a good number of hot-swap loaners so that kids are never without a functioning laptop.

NETWORK PERFORMANCE. The more we use laptops in our classrooms and at night in our dorms, the more we realize that our program is really about 1-to-1 access to our network. So we've had to make sure our network is robust and reliable. In 2003, we updated all of our network electronics to be fully switched, 100 Mbps (with gigabit uplinks). We also replaced all of our wireless access points with 802.11 g (54 Mbps) to gain network access speed.

INTERNET BANDWIDTH. We've struggled to keep up with the expectations of our users with regard to the size of our Internet pipe. They were so used to a dedicated cable modem or DSL connection at home, our pipe, which was originally just a T1, seemed small to them. Our first solution, and we still use this, was to install a packet-shaping appliance to "massage" the traffic and allow or squeeze it depending on its academic or recreational value. We've subsequently added more actual bandwidth. Most of our traffic is http traffic. We now have a dedicated business-level cable modem (6 megabits per second) that we use exclusively to pull http traffic. This is hooked to a Linux-based proxy server to also help maximize our productive use.

SECURITY, VIRUSES, AND NETWORK CONTROL. Wireless access adds another layer to our network complexity and opens us up to new security threats. In 2003, we redid our network's logical structure to install many more VLANs (e.g., one per building, wireless, etc.) for increased control. In addition, we use an authentication and control appliance to control access to our network via centralized log in and MAC-based access controls. We also use this to moderate client and port on/off times for bedtime. When viruses became the massive issue they are now, we started an anti-virus server for the students and supplied the licenses (Sophos). In addition, we also use the control appliance to automatically scan clients as they log onto our network and place them into Quarantine VLAN if they've failed to keep up-to-date with virus definition and other security updates.

SPAM. We installed a campus-wide spam filter appliance to help unclog our e-mail server (95% of what we get is spam). This comes with a user-based quarantine (they get e-mailed once a day with a list of their spam) and user-defined white-list.

INTERNET FILTER. Our school doesn't filter Internet content, but we do monitor activity. We use a product that looks at all Internet traffic, classifies it, and provides reports to an administrator as to the acceptability of the activity (as defined by our AUP).

STORAGE. Our kids store massive amounts of files. We just installed a SAN to hold all of it; we now have terabytes' worth of disk space. This doesn't cover DV movie files, however, which we store locally and back up to FireWire drives.

BACKUP. The more we store, the more we back up. We now back up to large hard disks, and then to tape from there. It takes a dedicated server and all day to do it!

RECREATIONAL USE. Like everyone else, we're struggling to come up with strategies to monitor and control recreational use, primarily chatting. We've made some areas of school, such as the library, chat free, using our firewall and packet-shaping appliance. However, the community hasn't yet electronically prohibited chatting or games at other times. While we tell students that they shouldn't be doing it in class or in evening study hall, we don't yet electronically whack them for it.

FORNEY (TEXAS) INDEPENDENT SCHOOL DISTRICT

Roger Geiger, director of technology at Forney ISD, offers these suggestions for 1-to-1 program start-ups:

1. Don't try to roll out the laptops during the first week of school. There's already too much going on.

2. In Forney, we pay for the insurance and parents pay a $250 deductible if the laptop is seriously damaged or lost. Parents are also responsible for all non-warranty damage up to $250. So far, after a year and a half, we've had no damage charges below $250.

3. It's important to decide where you'll secure laptops when not in use during PE, lunch, band, and so forth. If students don't need their laptops at home, where can they leave them at school? Our laptops are too big for most of our lockers. On our elementary campus, we've stationed mobile laptop carts in each classroom so that laptops can be locked up and charged. When we expand the laptop program to the secondary level, we'll need to come up with a similar solution.

4. Working with laptops can eat up class time if teachers aren't prepared—boot up, shut down, program glitches, and so forth. You need to decide how you'll provide classroom tech support.

5. What do you do when the laptop battery runs out? Even with extended life batteries, ours sometimes run out of juice by the end of the day, and there's no good place to charge all of them in a regular classroom. The mobile laptop carts are our current solution, but we may revisit this when we expand the program.

6. If you don't want students to load non-approved software to their laptops, you'll have to lock them down to make it impossible. But if they take their laptops home, they'll need to be able to load printer drivers and connect to their home ISP, so you have to remove the load restriction. How do you prevent them from loading the stuff you don't want them to load? At Forney, we've locked our laptops down completely this year, making the support situation much simpler. The students can't use their laptops to get on the Internet at home and can't load home printer drivers, but neither of these are necessary for using the electronic textbooks that we've loaded onto their computers.

Expert Advice

St. Thomas students get a laptop, a case, usually a USB drive, and a 3-year warranty covering accidental damage. It's non-negotiable. We give interested parents information about insurance specifically for laptop use and tell them to look into their own household insurance policies to see if they cover damage not considered accidental. They have to buy the always-on protective case we prescribe. This works out well: our vendor takes the orders and parents pay the vendor directly. The vendor ships the laptops here, and we image them. This is a lot easier, because they have built-in wireless cards.

— Elizabeth Cohen, St. Thomas School, Coral Gables, Florida

Conclusion

After reading about the myriad logistical issues that must be addressed when you add laptops to the mix of technologies at your school, you may be thinking that a laptop program is too daunting a proposition. But take heart. Adding laptops to your network will indeed increase its complexity and require strategic planning, extra time, and flexible, committed personnel, but what we've learned from the leaders of 1-to-1 programs around the country can help all of us succeed in rising to these challenges.

Part Three

TEACHING AND LEARNING IN A 1-TO-1 ENVIRONMENT

GIVING STUDENTS UBIQUITOUS ACCESS to computers changes the classroom learning environment in a variety of fundamental ways. For a laptop program to be successful, teachers need support and encouragement so that they can embrace those changes and modify their instructional practices and classroom management strategies.

Reflective teachers will find this to be a natural process—that of deconstructing familiar approaches in the light of new tools, resources, and theories of learning and then merging those theories with daily practice.

Ubiquitous access changes what teachers can do and expect, and it changes the way students can respond and engage. The chapters in part 3 will help you start making those changes so that you can take advantage of what 1-to-1 has to offer.

Previewing the Chapters

In Chapter 8, Donna DeGennaro surveys current research on how students learn and applies it to the 1-to-1 classroom. She offers teachers practical suggestions for making the most of this new learning environment. Dr. DeGennaro has bridged theory and practice throughout her career, having provided technology leadership and instruction at several Philadelphia schools. She has held research and teaching positions with several Philadelphia area colleges and is currently assistant professor of curriculum and teaching at Montclair State University in Montclair, New Jersey.

Chapter 9 looks at classroom management strategies for the 1-to-1 classroom: classroom setup, just-in-time technical support, loaner laptops, software for monitoring and managing the classroom, content filtering, policies and consequences, and a number of other management tips and ideas from laptop experts. The 1-to-1 classroom presents teachers with issues and challenges that non-laptop classrooms don't have, but thoughtful planning and flexible teaching can help you turn them into valuable benefits.

A sample lesson plan for a 1-to-1 classroom is offered in chapter 10. Elizabeth Cohen, director of technology at St. Thomas Episcopal Parish School in Coral Gables, Florida, shares a project-based lesson plan that is facilitated, enhanced, and extended through the use of laptop computers.

Chapter 8

CURRENT LEARNING THEORIES AND THE 1-TO-1 CLASSROOM

Donna DeGennaro

Introduction

ACCORDING TO the July 2005 PEW report *Teens and Technology: Youth Are Leading the Transition to a Fully Wired and Mobile Nation* (Lenhart, Madden, & Hitlin, 2005), young people increasingly use the Internet, interactive simulations, IM, and text messaging as a natural part of their everyday activities. While this study primarily reflects out-of-school technology uses, imagine what can happen when students are given 1-to-1, 24/7 access to laptop computers. The question becomes: how can educators effectively bridge out-of-school technology practices with in-school 1-to-1 laptop learning?

When it comes to technology, most of us have heard the familiar refrain, "Technology can facilitate good teaching and learning when used appropriately." But what does this really mean? We've read examples of effective technology integration, yet sometimes we still have trouble visualizing and explaining it, particularly in an environment where every student has a machine. We're left to ask ourselves: What's the relationship between good teaching and learning and how can technology be used appropriately to support these practices? What exactly *is* "appropriate use of technology"?

To begin to answer these questions and understand the value of 1-to-1 laptop learning, we must first take a look at current theories of how people learn and what this implies about the proper design of learning environments. Armed with this knowledge, we can then begin to consider how 1-to-1 laptops support these principles and implications and define appropriate uses for this technology resource.

Figure 8.1
Classrooms with laptops everywhere are de rigueur at The Urban School.

How People Learn

A seminal work titled *How People Learn* deftly summarizes current theories about learning and the design of learning environments (Bransford, Brown, & Cocking, 2000). This book reports on the ongoing efforts of cognitive scientists and educational researchers to explore the nature of learning. The work has resulted in the publication of a set of guiding principles about learning as well as the implications of those principles on the design of community-centered learning environments (see Table 1).

A new NSF-funded learning center known as LIFE (Learning in Informal and Formal Environments) is currently bringing together cross-disciplinary researchers to build on this work. The center's aim is to study the social, cultural, cognitive, and affective dimensions of learning and how transformative education technologies can support the principles reflected in Table 1 (Bransford, Brown, & Cocking, 2000).

TABLE 1. Guiding principles for learning and implications for learning environments.

PRINCIPLE	IMPLICATION
1 Students come to the classroom with preconceptions about how the world works. If their initial understanding is not engaged, they may fail to grasp the new concepts and information that are taught, or they may learn them for purposes of a test but revert to their preconceptions outside the classroom.	Schools and classrooms must be learner-centered
2 To develop competence in an area of inquiry, students must: (a) have a deep foundation of factual knowledge, (b) understand facts and ideas in the context of a conceptual framework, and (c) organize knowledge in ways that facilitate retrieval and application.	Schools and classrooms must be knowledge-centered
3 A "metacognitive" approach to instruction can help students learn to take control of their own learning by defining learning goals and monitoring their progress in achieving them.	Schools and classrooms must be assessment-centered
4 Learners' brains develop not in isolation, but rather as a function of social interactions with others in the environment.	Schools and classrooms must be community-centered

The terms *learner-centered, knowledge-centered, assessment-centered* and *community centered* can take on various meanings. Their distinct definitions in this context are important to explicate.

LEARNER-CENTERED ENVIRONMENTS

It's important to note first that "learner-centered" is distinct from "student-centered." Learner-centered environments focus on students' prior knowledge and experiences as well as their cultural backgrounds, because students come to the classroom with a particular understanding of how the world works. Educators can maximize student success by finding ways to uncover what students know and how they've come to know it.

In terms of technology, the significant questions are: What technology literacies do learners come with? How have previous and ongoing experiences with technology shaped their learning and communicational styles? How can we begin to tap this experience and knowledge in effective ways and make the best use of ubiquitous access?

KNOWLEDGE-CENTERED ENVIRONMENTS

Knowledge-centered environments focus on sense-making and deep understanding of concepts. A knowledge-centered activity provides students the opportunity to uncover the "big ideas" as they work on real-world problems and scenarios. Basic skills and factual knowledge develop within larger conceptual frameworks rather than through lecture and memorization.

In a knowledge-centered environment, students use meta-cognitive skills to "explore, explain, extend and evaluate their progress" (Bransford, Brown, & Cocking, 2000). Meta-cognitive skills are essential to fostering the kind of active exploration and application of knowledge that is needed to extend and transform students' initial preconceptions.

In terms of technology, the significant questions are: How does technology support and facilitate student knowledge development? How do continuously accessible technology applications foster student negotiation of meaning and deep understanding of information and concepts?

ASSESSMENT-CENTERED ENVIRONMENTS

Assessments can be formative or summative. Formative assessment engages students and teachers in a continual feedback loop, requiring both to reflect on the learning process that's taking place in the classroom. Teachers reflect on the observations they make of classroom activities and student performance on formative assessment tasks, while students reflect on their own learning process and performance or the learning process of a peer.

This type of meta-cognitive activity is most valuable when teachers and students use these reflections to revise their work and improve their performance. For teachers, this can come in the form of altered curricular designs or the use of new learning resources. Students can use this reflection to critique and revise their research questions and apply in new ways the information they've accumulated.

Summative assessments, on the other hand, provide a quantitative and qualitative picture of where students are at a particular point in their learning process. Summative assessments include tests, quizzes, portfolios, or other means of gathering information about student progress.

In terms of technology, the significant questions are: How can technology assist teachers in administering, scoring, and reflecting on formative and summative assessments? How does technology mediate students' ability to participate in their own (and their peers') ongoing formative assessments?

COMMUNITY-CENTERED ENVIRONMENTS

When we think of creating a classroom community, we often have images of establishing rules in order to have "good classroom management". While community-centered does refer to the norms and expectation of participation, it is more complex than this. For one, identified norms of participation should reflect the culture from which the students come. Different ways that students act at home and in their communities can directly impact how they will successfully participate in school. Another important aspect of community-centered environments is that they embody characteristics of Vygotsky's (1978) notion of social learning. This view requires creating classrooms that foster norms of interactions which allow learners to move from actual to potential developmental levels of understanding ("zones of proximal development") by working with others. In this view initial and evolving mental development becomes more visible when students have the opportunity to amiably share understandings, negotiate meaning as well as cordially reason and argue with each other (Darling-Hammond & Bransford, 2005).

In terms of technology, the significant questions are: How can technology be helpful in building effective community? How does technology support norms of sociable knowledge sharing, negotiation, reasoning and argumentation?

It's important to note that all four of these guiding principles focus primarily on *what is being learned* rather than *what is being taught*. These principles establish a conceptual framework that centers on what *students* are doing in the classroom rather than what teachers are doing. However, this should not be understood to imply that students must always work in groups, nor does it mean that students should never receive structured guidance from the teacher. From understanding and accommodating learners' backgrounds, to helping learners construct knowledge out of new information, to finding opportunities for continuous reflection and revision, this framework lays the groundwork for conceptualizing appropriate uses of technology that will support what we have learned about how people learn.

Using Technology to Support Learning

To begin our consideration of appropriate uses of technology, let's imagine a scenario that typifies how youth today interact with and co-opt the technology tools of our increasingly wired and mobile nation:

> A student, Kellie, is at home at her desk. Kellie's laptop is in front of her, her cell phone is to the side, and her iPod is nearby playing her favorite tunes. As she listens to the music, she types away on the laptop. She's not doing just one thing on the computer but several. Her IM window buzzes with messages and replies from six buddies chatting all at the same time, and several other windows sit open in the background. IM is currently the focus: she and her friends are discussing their fantasy football results for the week. They argue over who the best players are and who they'll choose next time. While still IMing, Kellie toggles back and forth between browser windows to investigate player stats, results from last week, and predictions for next week's games.
>
> As the conversation continues in IM, Kellie hears her phone buzz. Another friend is text messaging her to ask what she's up to. Kellie texts back and invites her friend to join the IM chat. Now she has seven buddies. Without missing a beat, Kellie and her friends continue to discuss the best configuration of players for the fantasy team. There are points of agreement and points of contestation. Regardless, they can immediately back up their opinions with facts gleaned from the Web (as well as their combined fantasy football experience). Playing Madden—a simulated football franchise, league and game—they come to understand all elements of the game in a very realistic way, which in turn informs their decisions on players.

This scenario illustrates some of the many ways that members of the millennial generation integrate technology seamlessly into their everyday lives to communicate, build and share knowledge, make decisions, and participate in social networks. These kids are natural multitaskers, and technology gives them the tools to do what comes naturally and pursue these many important activities simultaneously. To older generations, this kind of multitasking behavior may seem bewildering and pernicious, an endless series of distractions and diversions that feed on and reinforce kids' chronically short attention spans. But what is really happening here is that kids are assimilating the givens of our media- and technology-driven society and using them in their own ways to learn what they need to learn to navigate and take their place in that society.

Yes, they are learning—this isn't just play or socialization. In the informal, technology-mediated learning environment described in this scenario, the activities are learner-centered, knowledge-centered, assessment-centered and community centered. The scenario is learner-centered in that it's focused on the interests of the participants and depends upon and activates the knowledge and skills that the participants bring with them. It is knowledge-centered because these young people are actively searching for and applying information in a goal-driven process. It is assessment-centered in that the participants are constantly challenging each other and evaluating alternative approaches and perspectives, which naturally causes them to reflect on and rethink their own preconceptions. Finally, it is community-centered in that there are particular norms of social participation with technology that afford the girls an opportunity to negotiate their decisions about their players while at the same time raising the level of learning through the social process.

For many of us, it may seem quite a stretch to compare what happens in this informal learning environment to what happens (or should happen) in the more formal school learning environment. While it's true that this scenario says something important about the way kids use technology today to help them understand the way the world works, these kids aren't really building on or extending the kinds of conceptual frameworks that are implied by and necessary to academic learning, are they? These students are using new information and their own prior knowledge, but they aren't really gaining a deep comprehension of the topic or synthesizing it to make a compelling argument. Transcripts of this IM chat might reveal substantial reflection on and revision of previous ideas, yet these buddies may not be consciously reflecting on their personal learning or that of their peers.

But these are differences in degree, not in kind. At the most fundamental level, this scenario embodies most of the principles posited by current learning theories and can tell us much about effective and appropriate use of technology in a laptop-equipped classroom.

Bridging the Gap between Informal and Formal Learning Environments

This scenario can help us bridge the gap between the learning activities that young people naturally pursue at home and with their friends, and the learning environment that teachers create in the classroom. Let's take this same scenario and apply it to a 1-to-1 classroom setting.

In the description that follows, the teacher is engaging students in a project-based learning (PBL) activity. Project-based models are designed to immerse teams of students in the exploration of a real-world problem or issue. Students are required to build on their previous experience and knowledge to come up with a solution or create a product that they then present to others. These projects are self-directed and research-based and require students to collaborate and employ problem-solving skills. The end products or presentations should illustrate that students have extended their understanding by actively engaging with the subject matter and using the information they've gathered to create or communicate something new:

> Kellie is now in a 1-to-1 laptop classroom. As at home, she has many technologies and applications at her fingertips (whether that includes the cell phone or the iPod is something to consider for another time!). Instead of working with her peers from a distance, she now sits shoulder to shoulder with her classmates, who have their own laptops at hand. In addition to IM and Internet, Kellie and her classmates will use a variety of software programs in the process of completing this activity.

> The students are divided into groups to address a community problem: water pollution. They read stories about the rise in pollution levels and develop an inquiry question that will lead them in a search for the reasons behind this phenomenon.

> Kellie's group begins by assessing the situation. They study the details of the pollution reports and record questions they have. They use a graphic organizer program (such as Inspiration) to create a concept map of this information and to identify the "bid ideas" that frame these individual details. Each student in Kellie's group does this individually, and then they all use IM to negotiate the central problem and agree upon an inquiry question for their group.

> The teacher is "lurking" online, adding comments and questions and pushing groups to clarify their thinking. The teacher does this from a distance for several reasons: this allows her to listen in on each group more or less at the same time and discover what previous knowledge each student brings to the learning activity. It also permits her to save this initial "record" of student understanding for both formative and summative assessment. Based on their teacher's feedback, the student groups complete their concept maps and formulate their inquiry question.

> The next day, the students come in ready to begin the research process. They open the graphic organizer program on their laptops and review their concept maps. The teacher then introduces them to Artemis, an educational search engine designed to help students keep their inquiry question in mind as they pursue Web research. The students use their laptops to access Artemis and begin their search for information. A list of suggested Web sites organized by their teacher is available in the background.

> Students sit close to each other and share and interpret what they find (Distributed Cognition). This type of activity encourages the negotiation of current and constructed knowledge. The teacher interjects on occasion to ensure that students are clarifying what they've written and reflecting on how they've arrived at their proposed solution.

> To see the results of their suggested solution, the students use a simulation program (such as Model-It) that will allow them to see multiple representations of the data. Students enter the pollution data to bring the simulation to life. The simulation simultaneously illustrates data in pictures, graphs, and numbers and shows potential outcomes in multiple forms. Students draw conclusions about what they see and analyze the effectiveness of their

proposed solution by making connections between these multiple representations. Students determine if any missing pieces or additional information will be needed to complete their simulations.

The circle continues until the students come to the end of their allotted time. They close by using their laptops to create a final multimedia presentation that shares their findings with the class.

This scenario draws upon several learning theories and models of teaching. In this activity, learning is *distributed* (learning happens across people, tools, and artifacts), *situated* (learning is a social process that occurs in the context of a shared activity), and *constructed* (new learning is built from previous knowledge).

This is a project-based activity, but other teaching models will also work successfully in a 1-to-1 environment. Some of these teaching models include cognitive apprenticeship (Brown, Collins, & Duguid, 1989), case-based teaching (Schank, 1991), and anchored instruction (Bransford et al., 2000). (For more information see: www.edtech.vt.edu/edtech/id/models/)

The most important lesson to learn from this scenario is that rather than trying to apply *traditional* models of teaching to a 1-to-1 environment, we should look for ways to exploit ubiquitous access to make the learning environment more learner-, knowledge-, and assessment-centered. The flexibility laptops afford students gives them the ability to move in and out of applications as they organize the larger picture, agree upon the details, collaborate with their peers and teachers, and test solutions in ways not possible without interactive technologies.

The flexibility fostered by good instructional design in a laptop environment requires an enormous amount of responsibility on the part of both students and the teacher. Hand out the laptops without careful curricular planning, and students will find distractions for sure. However, if students are guided to use the tools in ways that emulate case-based scenarios, project-based learning, constructionist learning, anchored instruction, cognitive apprenticeship, and inquiry-based learning (Oliver, 2002), 1-to-1 laptops can have a strongly positive effect on learning.

A Final Thought

Technology can be both a benefit and a detriment to learning. It has been shown to be most beneficial when it's embedded in, and closely aligned with, curricular objectives and goals (Kulik, 2003). Moreover, technology use is most effective when it's used as a support for inquiry-based, problem-solving, and knowledge-construction activities (Oliver, 2002).

Some specific examples are

▶ computer-based animations and simulations that create multimodal opportunities for students and teachers to see, understand, and explain complex concepts;

▶ software tools that assist students in filtering and organizing data collected from the Internet; and

▶ Web-based applications that provide organizational support for online research within the context of previously designed inquiry activities that help learners solve real world problems.

Without this conceptual framework, technology has the potential of being used simply to perpetuate traditional forms of teaching and learning. In particular, students can be plugged into computers to do "drill and kill" tasks that aren't so different from those in traditional workbooks, and teachers can use multimedia technology to make their "sage on the stage" lectures more colorful and stimulating. Though there may be valid reasons to use such strategies in particular instances, these take little advantage of the great resources afforded by ubiquitous access (Bransford, Brown, & Cocking 2000).

In fact, when computers are used to reinforce low-level thinking skills, they can do more harm than good (Wenglinsky, 1998). The most appropriate uses of technology are those that align with current learning and models of teaching that incorporate what we have come to know about how people learn (see Table 2).

TABLE 2. Learning Theories and Models of Teaching.

LEARNING THEORIES (Kearsley, 2005; Papert, 1991)	
THEORY	DESCRIPTION
Affordance	Learning is guided by a "stimulus array": that is, the environmental setting provides clues necessary for the perception of what to do and how to do it. Learning environments should be realistic, unconstrained and provide perceptual cues.
Behaviorism (S-R)	Learning happens in discrete steps through carefully planned stimulus (questions) and response (reinforcement).
Constructionism	Learning occurs through the building of knowledge structures. The learner must be intentionally and actively engaged in constructing a product, which can be physical or abstract.
Constructivism	Learners engage in a continuous process of knowledge-building by using cognitive structures (mental models or schemas) as well as current or previous understandings to construct new ideas. The process includes hypothesizing, decision making, and knowledge transformation, and requires learners to engage with cases and context-bound problems.
Cognitive Flexibility	Learners are flexible, adaptable and have the means to instinctively reorganize knowledge under continuously changing circumstances.
Distributed Cognition	Learning happens across individuals, tools and artifacts in a given space. Tools and the organization of the tools are instrumental in how knowledge is shared and distributed.
Situated Cognition	Learning begins with activities and perceptions rather than abstract concepts. Further activity mediates the learner's conceptualization or cognition.
Situated Learning	Learning is an inherently social process that takes place within the context of social and cultural activity. This theory is grounded in Affordance and Social Development theories.
Social Constructivism	Students' previous knowledge and experience influences their social activity. Through this social activity, students draw upon their understanding of the world to create an understanding of what is considered "reality" or perceived as reality.
Social Development	Social interactions play an essential role in learning and the development of cognition. Learning happens first on the social level and then on the individual level. Moving from level to level depends upon the Zone of Proximal Development (ZPD). This theory builds on Social Learning theory.
Social Learning	Social learning refers to the interrelated and dialectical relationship between cognitive, behavioral and environmental components of a given situation. A key component to social learning is the observation and modeling of behaviors, attitudes and emotions of participants within the learning environment. Attention, memory and motivation are also essential components of social learning.
Radical Constructivism	Learning is constructed based on our mental schema and experiences of how the world works. Knowledge can only be constructed from that basis.

(continued)

TABLE 2. Learning Theories and Models of Teaching. *(continued)*

MODELS OF TEACHING	
MODEL	**DESCRIPTION**
Anchored Instruction	Anchored instruction draws upon situated cognition. Specifically, AI "anchors" students in realistic cases or problems. Students identify the problem and are given a specific role toward completing an assigned task. Students use information revealed through a story to find solutions. An example of this approach was developed by John Bransford and the Cognitive Technology Group at Vanderbilt University (Bransford, Sherwood, Hasselbring, Kinzer, & Williams, 1990). Using a series of video case studies, students work in groups to solve a problem. All of the information needed to solve the problem is provided in the structured video story.
Case-based Teaching	Case-based teaching finds its roots in both direct instruction and social constructivism. Teachers carefully structure the direction of activities and students work in groups to answer questions and negotiate decisions about the case. Both Roger Schank (www.engines4ed.org/hyperbook/misc/rcs.html) and Daniel Edelson (www.engines4ed.org/hyperbook/nodes/NODE-197-pg.html and http://josquin.cti.depaul.edu/~rburke/pubs/burke-kass-aaai94.pdf) have created model examples of such activities. In their examples, students are placed in a real-world case related to a specific topic or discipline. CBTs combine learner and knowledge-centered characteristics. Students draw on their past experience to answer questions and make decisions, but these past experiences are challenged when the system offers alternative solutions and when their classmates offer various interpretations of the case. Students are then required to research the case and use the information they gather to reconsider or support their position. Final decisions about the case are socially constructed and agreed upon. This implies that students must have a deep understanding of the content and be able to argue for the decisions they make and convince others that their particular solution is the best one.
Cognitive Apprenticeship	Cognitive apprenticeship is grounded in social constructivist learning theories. This model is also based on the concept of traditional apprenticeship: there is an expert and an apprentice. The teacher and learner role-shift throughout the learning process. The expert role can be played by the teacher, an outside expert, or a cognitive tutor (www.carnegielearning.com/products.cfm). The expert's job is to model real-world activities in a way that aligns with the apprentice/learner's ability level. Specifically, the expert uses modeling, coaching, and fading strategies, while helping the learner move from novice to expert. The apprentice observes the master, and copies her actions on a similar task. The expert coaches the apprentice through the entire process. Coaching takes the form of provided hints and corrective feedback as well as explicit explanations of how and why tasks are done in a particular way. As the apprentice becomes more skilled in the task, the master gives more and more authority to the apprentice by "fading" into the background. The learner needs to articulate mastered knowledge by talking through their thinking process and drawing upon shared knowledge in appropriate ways throughout the activity. In this way, the teacher assesses where the student is and how well they are internalizing new concepts and information to connect with meaningful learning.

(continued)

TABLE 2. Learning Theories and Models of Teaching. *(continued)*

MODELS OF TEACHING	
MODEL	**DESCRIPTION**
Constructionism	Constructionism falls between social and radical constructivist learning theories. Constructionism contends that students learn best by creating a physical or conceptual model. Rather than limiting this model-building to contexts or cases as in constructivist activities, students in a constructionist environment are responsible for creating their own problems. Students can work in teams or individually. Either way, in order for the students to succeed, they will need to continuously search for information and knowledge that can be applied to their problems. Students are ultimately responsible for justifying why and how they "build" things.
Goal-based Scenarios	Goal-based Scenarios is an instructional approach developed by Roger Schank. Grounded in situated learning and more instructor-directed than PBL, these structured computer simulations place the learner in an embedded instructional activity where learners take on a specific role to complete well-defined tasks and goals. These activities are learner-centered in that they are intended to be designed around student interests and knowledge. The expectation is that establishing this connection with the learner's interests will motivate them. GBSs are knowledge-centered because they require that students acquire and apply knowledge throughout supportive, scaffolded activities. Students move through simulations while simultaneously accessing the Internet to gather data, and keep electronic journals to record observations and reflections and apply the knowledge they have gained from each simulation.
Inquiry-based Models	Inquiry-based models require the learner to develop a question of personal interest. The learner then seeks data and knowledge that inform the question. The inquiry process continuously evolves through a cycle of raising questions, testing solutions, discovering what works and asking more questions to gain a deeper understanding of the problem at hand.
Project-based Models	In project-based models, teams of students explore real-world problems. Based in radical constructivism, students draw upon their own experiences and knowledge to eventually create a product or presentation that they share with others. These projects are self-directed and research-based, and require students to use problem-solving skills. The presentations should illustrate that students have called upon the knowledge of the world's best thinkers, and gathered and organized data into graphs, organizers and other effectively communicated representations.

References and Resources

Darling-Hammond, L., & Bransford, J. (2005). *Preparing teachers for a changing world: What teachers should learn and be able to do.* San Francisco, CA: John Wiley & Sons.

Bransford, J., Brown, A., & Cocking, R. (2000). *How people learn: Brain, mind, experience, and School.* Committee on Developments in the Science of Learning. Washington, DC: National Academy Press.

Bransford, J. D., Sherwood, R. D., Hasselbring, T. S., Kinzer, C. K., & Williams, S. M. (1990). Anchored instruction: Why we need it and how technology can help. In Nix, D., and Spiro, R. (Eds.), *Cognition, education, and multimedia*. Hillsdale, New York: Lawrence Erlbaum.

Brown, J. S., Collins, A., & Duguid, P. (1989). Situated cognition and the culture of learning. *Educational Researcher, 18* (1), pp. 32–41.

Cognition and Technology Group at Vanderbilt. (1990). Anchored instruction and its relationship to situated cognition. *Educational Researcher, 19* (5), pp. 2–10.

Kearsley, G. (2005). *Explorations in learning and instruction: The theory into practice database.* Retrieved September 29, 2005, from http://tip.psychology.org

Kulik, J. (2003). *Effects of using instructional technology in elementary and secondary schools: What controlled evaluation studies say.* Arlington, Virginia: SRI International. Retrieved March 30, 2005, from www.sri.com/policy/csted/reports/sandt/it/Kulik_ITinK–12_Main_Report.pdf

Lenhart, A., Madden, M., Hitlin, P. (2005). Teens and technology: Youth are leading the transition to a fully wired and mobile nation. Washington, DC: Pew Internet & American Life Project. Available from www.pewinternet.org/pdfs/PIP_Teens_Tech_July2005web.pdf

Papert, S., & Harel, I. (1991). *Situating constructionism.* Retrieved September 29, 2005, from www.papert.org/articles/SituatingConstructionism.html

Schank, R. C. (1991). *Case-based teaching: Four experiences in educational software design* (Tech. Rep. No. 7). Chicago, IL: Northwestern University, The Institute for the Learning Sciences.

Vygotsky, L. (1978). *Mind in society: The development of higher psychological processes.* Cambridge, MA: Harvard University Press.

Wenglinsky, H. (1998). Does it compute? *The relationship between educational technology and student achievement in mathematics.* Princeton, N.J.: ETS Policy Information Center.

WEB RESOURCES

Oliver, K. (2002). Teaching Models: www.edtech.vt.edu/edtech/id/models/

Using Cases in Teaching: http://tlt.its.psu.edu/suggestions/cases/

Case Study Teaching in Science: http://ublib.buffalo.edu/libraries/projects/cases/case.html

The Case-Based Teaching Architecture: www.engines4ed.org/hyperbook/nodes/NODE-196-pg.html

Concepts to Classroom: www.thirteen.org/edonline/concept2class/inquiry/

The Institute of the Learning Sciences: creANIMate: www.engines4ed.org/hyperbook/movies/crean.mov (imovie)

Learning in Informal and Formal Environments (LIFE) http://life-slc.org

Chapter 9

CLASSROOM MANAGEMENT STRATEGIES FOR 1-TO-1

Introduction

THERE'S NO DOUBT that teaching in a 1-to-1 classroom is different from teaching in a room without laptops. If there's a wireless network available, and if students have ready access to the Internet, e-mail, and all sorts of student-installed goodies, teachers are bound to encounter some classroom management challenges. But with a little planning, those challenges can be met, and the payoff can be truly astounding.

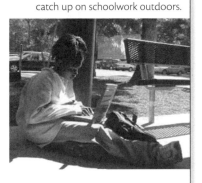

Figure 9.1
Students at Beaufort County School can catch up on schoolwork outdoors.

As always, the best defense is a good offense: if you can make what's happening in the classroom more interesting than what might be happening on the students' laptops, you'll have few problems keeping the students' attention. And that's what good teaching has always been about, anyway: what's going on in the classroom has to be more engaging and immersive than what's going on outside the window, or what's going on next door, or who just walked into the room, or any number of other interruptions and distractions. Laptops simply raise the ante somewhat. The teacher's task in a 1-to-1 environment is to structure projects and activities so that they're challenging, fun, and social—but not so social that only purposeless surfing and random messaging are taking place.

This chapter will introduce you to a number of management strategies used by laptop-using teachers—optimizing the setup of desks and tables, encouraging student collaboration, monitoring what's on the screens and keeping students on task, to name a few. These techniques and strategies will help you build a classroom environment that will be conducive to learning and social collaboration. As John Seely Brown has written (2001), "Learning is a remarkably social process. In truth, it occurs *not* as a response to teaching, but rather as a result of a social framework that fosters learning." The goal of this chapter is to help you create such a framework in your classroom.

Before the Students Arrive (P for Planning)

Some classroom management strategies can be put in place before students even take a seat. For instance, you can keep your 1-to-1 classroom running smoothly by

▶ making sure that technical support will be readily available when something goes wrong (and something *always* goes wrong, especially when you least expect it),

▶ placing desks and tables where they'll work best,

▶ determining where laptops will be stored and charged when not in use,

▶ having spare parts available when needed.

Lessons Learned

Videos from Veterans: Irving ISD

Irving Independent School District has interviewed some of their veteran laptop teachers and asked them to pass on their best classroom management techniques. New 1-to-1 teachers can learn much from these short videotaped interviews at www.irvingisd.net/one2one/classroom_management/cm_interviews.htm.

At The Peck School, students are told to charge their laptops overnight and bring them to school fully charged. However, we keep spare batteries charged and ready for those students who fail to do this. Spare power adapters are also available in the school's tech support office. Given our school's schedule—classes are divided into 40- and 60-minute blocks—most students find they can use their laptops throughout the day on a single charge. If they *do* need a recharge, power outlets in each classroom are designated for that purpose. Some schools find it useful to set up a special charging station area in classrooms, or even incorporate charging outlets into their laptop cubbies or cubicles.

Just-in-Time Technical Support

We've found that just-in-time technical support is a crucial component of classroom management. When—not if—computers have problems, fixing or replacing them right away can mean the difference between an integrated classroom and a disjointed one.

Peck is small enough that students and teachers are always close to the tech support office. Nevertheless, we outfit our technicians with walkie-talkies. When called, our network manager and technical support specialists stop whatever they're doing and come right away to fix problems. Teachers and students know they can leave their classrooms anytime and drop by our technical support area and either get a problem resolved quickly or walk back to class with a loaner laptop, battery, or power cord.

Room Setup

Room setup can go a long way toward determining the success of your 1-to-1 implementation. This is hardly news to educators, of course. More than 100 years ago, Dewey (1902, p. 31) pointed out the importance of classroom design when he related his struggle to find desks and chairs conducive to the kinds of learning activities he envisioned for his students.

We had a great deal of difficulty in finding what we needed, and finally one dealer... made this remark, "I am afraid we [do not have] what you want. You want something at which the children may work; these are all for listening."

Unfortunately, a full century later, we still have many classrooms set up for listening and not working. To get the most out of your laptop program, you need functional desks and seating arrangements that encourage student collaboration as well as teacher monitoring and facilitation.

Most of the laptop classrooms at Peck feature clustered seating and desk arrangements, allowing students to collaborate easily on projects and permitting teachers to circulate freely around the room. We're also planning a new computer lab for K–5 classes, which don't have their own laptops. We've decided to arrange the desks in either a double V or double U pattern, with plenty of space for teacher movement.

Some teachers have found it useful to teach from the back of the classroom, projecting the lesson, assignment, or PowerPoint presentation on the front wall while standing behind their students and monitoring laptop screens. This helps ensure students stay on task, and helps the teacher spot difficulties students might be having navigating to a Web site or using a function of their word processing or spreadsheet program.

Expert Advice

Furniture, A/C wiring, SmartBoards, and so forth, are important infrastructure considerations. We've moved toward flat-topped, rectangular desks as a replacement for the all-in-one chair/desk combos we previously had in many classrooms. We're adding SmartBoards to classrooms, and one day we'll probably have mounted projectors and SmartBoards in every classroom.

— Fred Bartels, Rye Country Day School, Rye, New York

Filtering and Logging Internet Use

Since Peck is a K–8 school, we filter and log all Internet use. Filtering keeps students away from questionable sites, and provides a teachable moment when students get "locked" from Internet access for repeated attempts to access a prohibited site. Once they're locked down, students have to come to the Technology Department to get unlocked, and we can talk to them about why the sites they tried to visit aren't appropriate. The practice of Internet filtering in schools has provoked a lot of blog traffic and commentary on free speech versus censorship themes. However, at Peck, there's not much controversy: since we teach younger age groups, nearly everyone at Peck supports filtering.

Logging Internet use is helpful for determining what a student did to get locked down, and it can also provide a way to see if students are straying from their appointed project during class time. If students are buying shoes or checking out the latest music video instead of working on a math project, that can be discovered fairly easily if you log all Internet traffic.

Software Solutions for Classroom Management

A number of new classroom management programs can help you manage your 1-to-1 classroom.

If monitoring every student's screen is important to you, consider the Apple Remote Desktop (ARD) for Apple computers. This program has an easy-to-use interface and allows any user with an administrator's license to view any client computer on the network. It's even possible to view several client screens at the same time. We install the ARD client on all student computers and tell students they may *not* delete the software. We use ARD judiciously, primarily in situations where students are doing independent research online and may be tempted to do a little off-task surfing or shopping.

Similar programs are available for PCs, including Discourse and DyKnow, both of which offer features in addition to remote desktop monitoring. For example, DyKnow Monitor allows administrative users to call up screen snapshots of client computers, lock client keyboards and mice, and black out client screens on command. It can also be used to control access to specific software on client computers, preventing your class of eighth-graders from using their Web browser when they're supposed to be filling in data on their spreadsheets, for instance.

CLASSROOM MANAGEMENT THROUGH INTEGRATED SOFTWARE AND TEACHER TRAINING MODELS

Bruce Montgomery of Michigan's Freedom to Learn (FTL) laptop program (see chapter 3) reports that Michigan has contracted with several professional development providers to offer teachers ongoing training in technology integration and classroom management techniques. These programs include:

NTeQ Model (www.nteq.com): Integrating Computer Technology into the Classroom. In this program, FTL teachers receive systematic skill development training in specific technology integration techniques. The NTeQ model focuses on student-centered, problem-based teaching and learning. "Supercoaches" serve as statewide trainers of the NTeQ model and share their technology expertise with FTL teachers.

Intel Teach to the Future (www.macul.org/mirta/). This is a suite of free professional learning opportunities for teachers and administrators focusing on technology integration in the classroom. Two 40-hour courses for teachers ("Essentials Course" and "Workshop on Teaching Thinking with Technology") and a 4-hour "Leadership Forum" for administrators are available.

The ATA Technology Academy (http://ataacademy.org). This team-based program focuses on curriculum integration of technology, especially in individual school buildings. ATA has developed four special workshops to help FTL teachers and media specialists with the integration process.

Bringing the Wandering Sheep Back to the Fold

A typical challenge for 1-to-1 teachers is dealing with Internet "wanderers." No matter how engaging, social, and fun your lessons and projects may be, students with a live Internet connection will still be tempted to drift off to parts unknown. This can be dealt with in several ways.

At the 2004 Lausanne Laptop Institute, I learned a terrific technique called "Stick 'em Up." Dan Hudkins of the Harker School in San Jose, California, told us that whenever Harker teachers begin to suspect that their students' attention (and browsers) are wandering, they simply pull out their five-fingered six-shooter and say, "Stick 'em up!" Students must immediately put their hands in the air, allowing the teacher to walk around and check screens. Students who hesitate to raise their hands are checked more thoroughly. Judiciously used, this can help you identify and deal with those incorrigible Internet free rangers.

A similar and less punitive technique is "lids down," in which the teacher simply tells students to put the lids of their laptops down. Other teachers use the "fist rule." Students are instructed to lower their computer screens to about fist height—too low to look at without a lot of obvious scrunching down, but not totally closed. This method isn't entirely foolproof, as Cheryl Brockman of the St. Paul Academy and Summit School in St. Paul, Minnesota, reports (personal communication, January 21, 2006): "In the beginning, we would try to be kind and ask the students to 'lower their lids.' Most would, but eventually those little hands were able to sneak back under a fairly low lid and begin typing on something rather 'non-academic.' Now, we say 'lids down and I need to hear the click,' so that we can be sure that all lids are completely closed."

Speak Less, Facilitate More

Active, student-centered teaching and learning offers its own built-in classroom management benefits. When students know what to expect and what's expected of them, more work can be accomplished.

In my tech class at Peck, students know the structure of every session. We start the day by discussing what we're going to do, I answer any question, and then I send students off to do the work. I circulate during the class period, observing and interceding as needed. At the end of class, we usually get back together as a group to discuss what we've done.

In the lower grades, basic skills are stressed in the beginning. I walk around and view students' work and check that they save their work to the right location and under the right name. Students know that if they don't listen carefully at the start of class, they won't get their hands on their laptops as quickly. So they have a strong incentive to be on task right from the beginning. Taking advantage of students' inherent motivation to use the technology helps to get them to the learning and thinking more quickly.

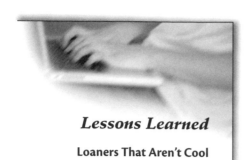

Training Students on Laptop Care, Procedures, and Expectations

Students need to be given some training on the proper care and feeding of their equipment: how to charge the batteries, how to carry laptops back and forth to school, how to lock them up, what to do when something goes wrong, and so forth. A good laptop orientation session at the beginning of the year, reinforced with a refresher course during the middle of the year, will help ensure they're cared for properly.

At Peck, we spend a lot of time teaching students how to put laptops into their cases and lock them securely in the cubbies. They're told to carry their laptops *in their cases* whenever they're walking *anywhere*—between classes, to the bus stop, at home, *anywhere*. Even in the classroom, carrying a laptop for any distance without its case is a recipe for disaster. As we've already noted, many schools have opted to use always-on cases to help prevent damage.

Policies and Consequences

It's the nature of students to test the boundaries that adults set for them. Rules for school computer usage are no exception. Students will push the envelope with their laptops just as they will with respect to the rules governing any other school property or program. It's important to plan for these transgressions and have specific policies and consequences in place.

You should have an Acceptable Use Policy that describes what everyone in your school or district may or may not do with regard to computers. Peck's LARK agreement, which states that all student computer usage must be **L**egal, **A**ppropriate, **R**esponsible, and **K**ind, is covered in chapter 7. Students are required to sign the LARK agreement as well as a full AUP, which goes into even more depth on these elements of appropriate technology use. The consequences for failure to observe the LARK rules range from a stern warning, to loss of computer privileges, to suspension, to expulsion from school.

The Best Defense...

Designing lessons specifically for the 1-to-1 classroom, and making these activities and projects fun, absorbing, and interactive, will head off the vast majority of classroom management challenges. Thoughtful curricular design and regular, ongoing reflection on student responses and performance are always the best ways to ensure effective teaching and learning.

Millennials who are interested in the work they're doing and invested in the project at hand are far more likely to stay on task. The wise teacher plans ahead and uses multiple classroom management strategies to keep students engaged. In this regard, teaching in a 1-to-1 classroom is no different from teaching in a non-laptop classroom. Reflective, well-planned teaching always wins out in the end.

Lessons Learned

Loaners That Aren't Cool

Every year Peck holds a few "loaner" laptops in reserve just in case students lose or damage the computer they've been issued. These older laptops aren't nearly as cool as the sleek, beautiful iBooks that all seventh- and eighth-grade students get at the start of the year. Instead, they're clunky, heavy clamshells, fully functional but totally lacking the cachet of iBooks. These clunky loaners provide students with a strong incentive to take good care of their laptops.

Chapter 10

TEACHING WITH LAPTOPS— A MODEL LESSON

Introduction

STUDENTS WITH 24/7 ACCESS to a digital assistant benefit in many ways. They can complete schoolwork both in class and at home. Their research, writing, calculations, presentations, and problem solving are likely to be better organized, more thorough, and more polished. The work they do is more readily available for timely and useful formative assessment. Given the comfort level with technology that is typical of this multitasking generation of millennials, it makes perfect sense for schools to provide students with the best tools available for the work they need to do.

Where investment in laptops really pays off is in the daily work of the classroom that teachers and students engage in together. When a teacher embraces 1-to-1 and works it into every aspect of the curriculum, new worlds of learning open up in ways never before imagined. Technology as a means to deepen and enhance every aspect of instruction—the vision that so many of us have had for so many years—is finally within reach. However, integrating laptops into day-to-day schoolwork is neither automatic nor easy. Teachers need both time and guidance to assimilate and experiment with new techniques and approaches before they can become fully competent and confident in a 1-to-1 environment.

Early in my education career, I worked for the Fieldston School in Riverdale, New York. I had no teaching experience then but was hired to run the computer network and provide technical support. One day, an experienced teacher of English invited me to visit her classroom. When I arrived, they were discussing *Huckleberry Finn*. I remember sitting spellbound as she led the discussion, amazed at how many instructional functions she was able to perform and accomplish at the same time: facilitating, coaching, encouraging, restating, energizing, persuading, questioning, summarizing, listening, and leading everyone, myself included, to a greater

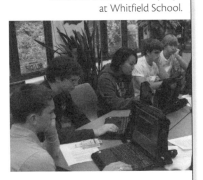

Figure 10.1
Students work on their laptops at Whitfield School.

understanding of the book. It was the first time I was made fully aware of what a master teacher can do in the classroom.

Teachers may worry that this kind of intuitive rapport with their students will only be made more difficult when everything gets mediated through technology. But my experience at Peck, as well as the experience of the other 1-to-1 pioneers interviewed for this book, has proved to me that this kind of teaching is eminently possible in a 1-to-1 classroom. With reflective practice and support, teachers can learn to be more engaging and masterful than ever before.

When I worked at Fieldston, I saw many examples of fine teaching. Even in those classrooms where the teacher was in front and students faced forward, the learning environment did not *feel* teacher-centered. Every student voice had validity and authority and contributed something to the discussion. Teachers were unafraid to shift roles—from authority, to witness, to facilitator, to learner, and back again—at any point in the discussion. It's this flexibility of approach that's crucial to teaching in a room full of laptops.

We've all heard the "sage on the stage" versus the "guide on the side" debate so many times that it's become an easily ignored cliché. I would argue, however, that in a 1-to-1 classroom, this debate is stood on its head to a considerable degree. In a 1-to-1 classroom, we're all sages because we all have access to every conceivable fact or resource that we'll ever need. They're right at our fingertips. And in a 1-to-1 classroom, we're *all* potentially guides on the side, sharing what we know and learning what we don't in an ongoing collaboration. The teacher who can embrace these possibilities and let go of the fear of not knowing all there is to know about the technology will be the one to succeed in a 1-to-1 environment.

Rethinking Curriculum When Resources Are Distributed

One of the first things teachers realize when planning lessons or projects for a 1-to-1 classroom is that learning resources are now distributed and don't have to be doled out. This can eliminate a whole lot of front-end planning about who uses what, how, and when. Everyone with a laptop has equal access to the Internet, the school's computer network, printers and presentation tools, and online research databases and search engines. It's almost impossible to overemphasize how this changes curricular planning: there's no more "who uses the reference books first" or "what do the others do while the reference books are being used." Instead, teachers and students can get right to the more important issues of problem solving, synthesizing, evaluating, and presenting.

My personal approach is to get students' hands on a project as quickly as possible. The students I teach seem to need less "chunking" than students used to; in other words, they don't need me to disassemble an idea or assignment and have them reassemble it later. Instead, they seem to prefer either onscreen highlights or electronic instructions (sent by e-mail) that they can act on right away. This approach supports differentiation in a simple but powerful way: students can immediately tackle the assignment in whatever way works best for them rather than following a series of prescribed steps and waiting for others along the way. Easy differentiation is one of the major potential benefits of 1-to-1, as highlighted in the model lesson that follows.

Differentiated Learning with Laptops

Staff members at St. Thomas Episcopal Parish School in Coral Gables, Florida, know a good deal about differentiated learning. They've invested many hours collectively exploring how this approach can help their students. Students come to St. Thomas with varying educational experiences, learning styles, and developmental readiness. How can teachers reach every student in the classroom when students vary so widely in their abilities and inclinations? Where do you place the bar when you want your school to be challenging but not daunting? The teachers at St. Thomas have decided that differentiated learning—enabled and enhanced by technology—can be a key to meeting all of their students' needs. The following lesson demonstrates how laptops can be used to differentiate instruction and support student success.

Model Lesson
THE STUDY OF LIFE IN ANCIENT MESOPOTAMIA

Elizabeth Cohen, Director of Technology
St. Thomas Episcopal Parish School, Coral Gables, Florida

CONTENT AREA: Social Studies

GRADE LEVEL: Sixth Grade

UNIT DESCRIPTION: In this unit, students work in teacher-assigned groups to research and report on all phases of life in ancient Mesopotamia. Within each group, specific research tasks are differentiated by complexity: one student studies irrigation and farming (the least complex area), another student studies occupations, and another studies laws and religion (the most complex area). Each student is given a series of guiding questions to answer, and the group leader must see to it that each member of the group submits a complete set of answers for the group notebook. Once the group has finished with this task, group members work together to construct a model of an ancient Mesopotamian city that physically represents what they've learned through their research.

At intervals during the course of this project, all students who are studying a particular area (such as irrigation and farming) meet to discuss their guiding questions and what they've discovered. Using a projector, students share their answers and compare them for completeness and accuracy. Information, Web links, and suggestions for revision can be exchanged by e-mail. In this way, students become "experts" in their particular area and then "jigsaw" back to their original project group to teach the other members about their specialty.

TECHNOLOGY TOOLS: Laptop computers, wireless network with filter, Internet, classroom LCD projector with wireless access, printers

TECHNOLOGY SKILLS

☐ Students are expected to do Internet searches independently, authenticate information, and cite sources properly.

☐ Students must demonstrate independent use of applications such as e-mail, Word, Word tables, and spell checker.

☐ Students must demonstrate that they're able to connect, through the wireless device in their room, to the classroom projector.

☐ Students must demonstrate use of print screen, copy and paste, formatting tools, and draw and paint tools.

WEB-BASED AND PRINTED RESOURCES: All instructions and guiding questions are posted on the school's Web site along with a few Web links to jump-start the students' research (see www.stepsmia.org, Student Resources > sixth grade > Mesopotamia).

Figure 10.2
The main page for this project, www.stepsmia.org/mesopotamiab/.

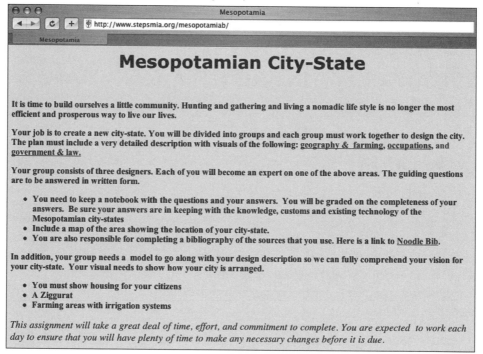

Students are encouraged to use Google's highlighter tool to assist their search. They are also directed to look at other classroom materials, magazines, maps, and books from the library about ancient Mesopotamia.

Figure 10.3.
Guiding questions for the "Irrigation and Farming" research area.

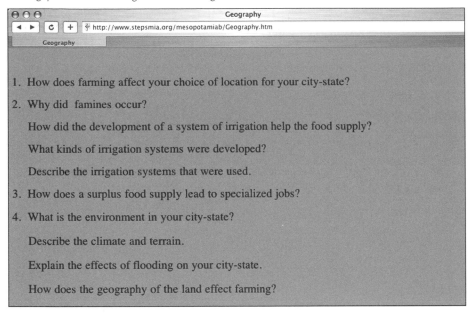

ACTIVITY SEQUENCE

The teacher begins this unit with a series of direct instruction classes about ancient Mesopotamia and the Fertile Crescent, after which students take an open book test assessing their general knowledge (see Figure 10.4). Some of the questions are factual, while others are open-ended; this is another way to differentiate the lesson. While the rest of the unit is almost entirely collaborative, no collaboration is allowed during tests.

As students learn about this topic and discuss the project with their group, they should keep a digital notebook to record their guiding questions and answers. During the project, task groups should periodically come together to discuss these questions. All resources must be cited correctly using NoodleTools' NoodleBib. Sources that cannot be authenticated, or are not cited, may not be used.

After the notebook is completed, students use found materials to create a model of an ancient Mesopotamian city. Each group presents its model and findings to other faculty and administrators on a scheduled "Ancient Mesopotamia" day.

At the end of the lesson unit, students take a final test on the core curriculum. The test is used as a summative assessment and is generally very similar to the quiz taken earlier (see Figure 10.4), but it's taken with books closed rather than open.

Lessons Learned

NoodleBib

NoodleTools' NoodleBib is an example of online technology that has made much simpler an activity that used to be far more complicated and troublesome for students—creating accurate bibliographical citations. While accurate citation is still crucially important and something that students need to learn and understand, with resources such as NoodleTools they no longer have to type in the references themselves and follow all the arcane rules specified by the various stylesheets. This saves them time and energy and results in more accurate citations.

Figure 10.4.
The Fertile Crescent Quiz.

THE FERTILE CRESCENT QUIZ

Name

Open Homework/Outline

Explain the meaning of the name "Fertile Crescent." What does each word mean in describing this region? (8 pts.)

What are the 2 major rivers in Mesopotamia? (8 pts.)

Explain the relationship between the following words: farming, drought, famine, flood, irrigation, surplus, and specialization and trade. (27 pts.)

Why are Sumerian cities called "city-states"? (4 pts.)

What was a ziggurat and what was its purpose? (8 pts.)

Why did Sumerians begin to use cuneiform? (4 pts.)

What was the Code of Hammurabi and why is it important to history? (8 pts.)

What religion did the ancient Hebrews begin to develop? (4 pts.)

What 3 major religions come from the family of Abraham? (9 pts.)

Describe 2 things that Moses did. (8 pts.)

What is the difference between polytheism and monotheism? (8 pts.)

For what was Solomon known? (4 pts.)

Why Laptops Enhance This Lesson

1-to-1 laptops allow each student in the classroom to research, communicate, write, draw, plan, and present their findings simultaneously, using the same set of tools at the same time—no waiting or sharing.

Laptops support differentiated learning because students can be grouped in a variety of ways and can work at their own pace, with their own learning styles. The project is challenging, fun, and collaborative, and laptops are the perfect vehicle for connecting and combining all the individual pieces of work being done by each student.

This constructivist project gets kids engaged and excited about customizing their own end product, giving them ample opportunity to exercise higher order thinking and problem-solving skills. In the end, every member of each group has a chance to be an expert and present to, and learn from, the other members, leading to greater learning for all.

Assessment Rubrics

SKILLS RUBRIC—GROUP PROJECT				
GRADE	A	B	C	D
Working with Others	Almost always listens to, shares with, and supports the efforts of others. Tries to keep people working well together.	Usually listens to, shares with, and supports the efforts of others. Does not cause waves in the group.	Often listens to, shares with, and supports the efforts of others, but sometimes is not a good team member.	Rarely listens to, shares with, or supports the efforts of others. Often is not a good team player.
Contributions	Routinely provides useful ideas when participating in the group and in classroom discussion. A definite leader who contributes a lot of effort.	Usually provides useful ideas when participating in the group and in classroom discussion. A strong group member who tries hard.	Sometimes provides useful ideas when participating in the group and in classroom discussion. A satisfactory group member who does what is required.	Rarely provides useful ideas when participating in the group and in classroom discussion. May refuse to participate.
Focus on the task	Consistently stays focused on the task and what needs to be done. Very self-directed.	Focuses on the task and what needs to be done most of the time. Other group members can count on this person.	Focuses on the task and what needs to be done some of the time. Other group members must sometimes nag, prod, and remind to keep this person on task.	Rarely focuses on the task and what needs to be done. Lets others do the work.
Effort	Work reflects this student's best efforts.	Work reflects a strong effort from this student.	Work reflects some effort from this student.	Work reflects very little effort on the part of this student.

SKILLS RUBRIC—NOTEBOOK

GRADE	A	B	C	D
Notebook	Notebook has been completed and shows clear, logical relationships between all topics and subtopics.	Notebook has been completed and shows clear, logical relationships between most topics and subtopics.	Notebook has been started and includes some topics and subtopics.	Notebook has not been attempted.
Quality of Information	Information clearly relates to the main topic and provides several supporting details and/or examples.	Information clearly relates to the main topic and provides 1–2 supporting details and/or examples.	Information clearly relates to the main topic, but no details and/or examples are given.	Information has little or nothing to do with the main topic.
Organization	Information is very organized, with well-constructed paragraphs and subheadings.	Information is organized, with well-constructed paragraphs.	Information is organized, but paragraphs are not well-constructed.	The information appears to be disorganized.
Mechanics	No grammatical, spelling, or punctuation errors.	Almost no grammatical, spelling, or punctuation errors	A few grammatical, spelling, and punctuation errors.	Many grammatical, spelling, and punctuation errors.

SKILLS RUBRIC—CITY-STATE MODEL

GRADE	A	B	C	D
Model Construction	Model is constructed of appropriate materials and demonstrates the students' pride in construction. Construction problems are solved. Model is completed on time.	Good choices are made in choosing material and display the students' creativity. Persistence is shown while problem solving. Model is turned in on time.	Model looks similar to descriptions; however, some features are not supported by the research.	The materials are poorly chosen. When troubles occur, problem solving is absent. Model is not turned in on time.
Accuracy	Model is created accurately. It shows many added details that make it come to life.	Model is created to look similar to the descriptions found during research. Imaginative details are added.	Information clearly relates to the main topic, but no details and/or examples are given.	Model has little or nothing to do with the topic.
Research	Bibliography shows many research references used in planning the model.	Bibliography shows some of the references used in planning the model.	Bibliography shows a few of the references used in planning the model.	No bibliography is included.

Conclusion

LOOKING TO THE FUTURE
OF UBIQUITOUS COMPUTING

HERE IS A SHORT TRANSCRIPT of an IM chat between two Peck School seventh-graders discussing the question, "What is the future of laptops in schools?"

> **Student 1 (10:26:22 PM):** watches
>
> **Student 2 (10:26:32 PM):** watches?
>
> **Student 1 (10:26:57 PM):** that have pop up holographic screens
>
> **Student 1 (10:27:19 PM):** touch screens
>
> **Student 2 (10:27:39 PM):** oh come on...seriously...like in the near future, do you think that all schools will have laptops and they'll become something like textbooks, or what do you think?
>
> **Student 1 (10:28:08 PM):** hmmmm...
>
> **Student 1 (10:29:02 PM):** i think that by the time every student in every school has an iBook, we'll have the watches
>
> **Student 1 (10:31:21 PM):** i wonder if they'll make edible electronics?

This somewhat funny exchange is included here for several reasons. First, it's to show that instant messaging, despite its rather free and easy approach to grammar and spelling, is certainly not the "bane of the English language" that it's sometimes reported to be. Instead, it's a natural forum of communication for the millennial generation, where kids feel empowered to discuss and debate ideas both big and small.

More important, though, it's to demonstrate that the future is forming right now in the dreams and ideas and expectations of our students, and that we as adults need to listen to what they're saying and thinking or we'll be left far behind. This is the reality we're tacitly acknowledging when we speak of "digital natives" and "digital immigrants": kids growing up in today's digital, networked environment are different from us. They've grown up in a different place and culture. They think differently, learn differently, and communicate in a technology-mediated "creole" that doesn't easily translate into the language of their digital immigrant parents and teachers. If we hope to understand what the future of ubiquitous computing might look like, the best place to start might be to ask our kids.

With that in mind, here are some more interesting and thoughtful responses to the same question:

Student A (10:44:05 PM): what do you think the future of laptops in schools is?

Student B: umm...laptops that have unlimited memory and wireless is available everywhere

Student A (10:50:19 PM): cool

Student A (10:51:15 PM): so pretty much, not having the limits that restrain our use of laptops today

Student B (10:51:27 PM): yeah

Student A (10:51:36 PM): awesome idea

Student B (10:53:34 PM): like all memory could be shared on the Internet, so there's this huge amount of memory that everyone has access to. So if one person has more memory than they need, their computer will give the memory out to the worldwide server and someone else who needs it can have it

Student A (10:54:33 PM): that would be cool...but then i guess you'd pay for the memory you got off the Internet

Student A (10:54:40 PM): and there would be a very delicate balance of worldwide memory...

Student B (10:57:33 PM): well, yeah but 1) we would all pay an up-front premium price for sharing memory and 2) the system would be so tested and perfected that the balance would be preplanned

Student A (10:57:46 PM): wow

Student A (10:57:50 PM): huge project

Student B (10:58:13 PM): also, the system would be broken up into several divisions so that the entire thing was never down

It's fascinating to see how these seventh-graders are exploring the possibilities of our interconnected, digital world—sharing limited resources and learning to work together with people all over the world. Clearly, for these seventh-graders, the world is already *flat*.

No doubt about it, planning for this new, flat world at the school or district level is a difficult challenge. Schools are goal-oriented, consensus-driven, thoughtful, and cautious institutions not given to rapid change. Technology, on the other hand, is constantly changing, interactive, and prone to 180-degree shifts and early obsolescence. Technology planning, therefore, is an extremely tricky and complex process: the technology has often moved on before the ink on the latest 5-year plan is dry. In response, many schools are now going to 2- or 3-year technology plans so that they can react faster to the latest technology innovations.

While no one can say with any certainty what education technology will look like 5 or 10 years from now, we can still

Expert Advice

There is a great need for software that allows students to creatively explore and play with the various knowledge domains taught in schools. We need a Physics Sketchpad, a Chemistry Sketchpad, a Biology Sketchpad. In other words, we need computer-based manipulatives for *all* subjects taught in school. When they've finally been created and embraced by teachers, school will become a much more enjoyable and humane environment for all.

— Fred Bartels, Rye Country Day School, Rye, New York

hazard some guesses based on what's already happening in the field. From this digital immigrant's perspective, these are the trends that seem most likely to continue:

▶ Tablet PCs will continue to proliferate, and other major hardware vendors will enter the fray, bringing prices down. Tablet PCs will become smaller and more durable for the educational market. The number of specialized programs designed for Tablet PCs will increase, supporting constructivist teaching practices and hands-on applications.

▶ Handhelds will get larger while laptops and Tablet PCs get smaller. A form factor will emerge somewhere in the middle that will offer the ideal weight, configuration, durability, and price to make mobile computing accessible to every school and household.

▶ Broadband Internet access will become available and affordable for nearly all households, eliminating much of the current digital divide. Wireless and satellite-based Internet service will fill in access gaps in rural areas. Some schools today are already broadcasting Internet signals to their entire school district by means of wireless towers.

▶ Instant messaging will continue to grow, and savvy teachers will discover how to integrate these communication tools in educationally useful ways. Network managers will get better at eliminating their noneducational uses.

▶ Streaming audio and video, Web-based videoconferencing, podcasting, and other Web-based applications and technologies will proliferate in a Web 2.0 world.

▶ Textbook publishers will fully embrace e-book distribution models, making back-breaking book bags a thing of the past. Books will still be available in the classroom and school library for those who prefer to read from paper.

▶ Eventually, all networking will be outsourced. A utility bill will be paid every month for access to the Internet as well as shared, off-site databases and large-scale server farms. Pricing will be based on the services requested, including Internet screening and filtering. There will still be a need for school-based tech support people, but only for the desktop hardware, not for the network.

This just scratches the surface of what may be possible in the coming few years, but what a different educational landscape these changes portend!

Expert Advice

We're coming to a time—probably sooner than later—when kids will carry their own laptops or portable computers wherever they go. They'll probably be something like today's Palm or PocketPC, but far more capable. They'll carry them like they now carry cell phones, and use them just as regularly. Schools will provide network infrastructure—servers, printers, etc.—but not basic equipment. I think our days of providing machines are numbered.

I believe we should be very careful about extending out complex tech plans that require funding for machinery. We should instead put that funding into providing wireless access. Even faculty and staff will soon prefer their own portable machines to the hardware that schools provide.

— Catherine Meany, Boston Latin School, Boston, Massachusetts

1-to-1, Nationwide

To anticipate the future, it's important to have a solid sense of what's happening in the present. Up to now, that's been difficult to do with 1-to-1. But that's about to change. We'll soon learn the results of a national survey of 1-to-1 programs that was nearing its conclusion as this book went to press. First announced in eSchoolNews early in 2006 (www.eschoolnews.com/news/showStory.cfm?ArticleID=6060&page=2), this extensive survey is targeting key individuals in ubiquitous technology programs around the country. It will cover both existing 1-to-1 programs and those schools and districts planning to start similar programs in the next 5 years. The survey is being conducted by Jeanne Hayes of the Hayes Connection and Tom Greaves of the Greaves Group and is sponsored by current partners Pearson Education and Discovery Education. I spoke with Dr. Greaves as the survey was just getting underway and asked him to give a preview of his research approach and focus.

Greaves began by noting the current lack of data on laptop programs in the United States (personal communication, January 30, 2006):

> There is no repository of everything that is being done…Nationally, there are many unanswered questions. Even those in the best position to name laptop programs seem to be aware of only a handful of the one-to-one programs.

Greaves spoke about a ubiquitous computing committee in California that he had recently served on which included both public school personnel as well as several major hardware vendors. While each vendor was able to name its own programs, no one had any real awareness of other programs, nor was anyone trying to learn from others' successes and failures. Moreover, no broad-based study of 1-to-1 laptop schools existed for this group to review. This lack of information was the driving force behind the current study that Greaves and Hayes have undertaken.

MIT'S OLPC PROJECT AND THE $100 LAPTOP

The One Laptop Per Child program being pursued by MIT has certainly gotten the attention of all major hardware vendors, not all of it complimentary. While the final specifications for the $100 laptop are still being developed, it's very likely that OLPC will eventually lead to new hardware designs and lower prices for everyone. If this happens, we'll see smaller, better, and more affordable laptops for education—a win for us all!

Even within a state or district, the ways that 1-to-1 can be delivered and used often differ from school to school and classroom to classroom (ibid.):

> The actual implementation of 1-to-1 schools is highly variable. I went to one Maine school where the English teacher handed out printed assignments, asked students to go to a single Web site to do research, and then write up a report and hand it in on paper. This, to me, is not a particularly effective use of the tremendous resources that 1-to-1 can offer. The math teachers at this school hardly used the laptops at all. Even in a "state of the art" 1-to-1 program like Maine's, then, it seems that very few people have put together the "people" side of it all.

Another interesting thing he noted in the survey's early returns are the different ways that schools and districts have started their 1-to-1 initiatives (ibid.):

> A lot of people want to start their 1-to-1 programs with a full-building implementation, but others have started with just one grade. Unfortunately, if you limit it to just one grade, the school administration often seems reluctant to buy in.

This tends to support his view that the single biggest factor in a successful laptop implementation is administrative support and leadership.

Most of the district leaders and policymakers he had spoken to are focused on the future and where education technology is going in the next 5 to 10 years (ibid.):

> School districts and states are getting ready to spend large amounts of money—millions, perhaps even billions for a statewide program—so they want to know where the world is going.

He also heard this refrain from hardware vendors. While school leaders and legislatures are asking vendors to ramp up production so that they can take advantage of the economies of scale, vendors are coming back with the question "How do we know you will really buy a million of them?" They point to examples like that of Cobb County (Georgia), where a large district order for laptops was pulled at the last minute because of a legal challenge to the program's funding formula.

Capturing these intersecting interests and perspectives is a major goal of this survey, which asks pointed questions about how much districts plan to spend on 1-to-1 technology in the next 5 years and what their timeframe for purchase and adoption is (ibid.):

> We have included items on where districts might start, at which grade levels, what platforms they are considering, what changes they plan in the curriculum, what types of professional development will be included, etc. Altogether, we came up with 238 questions.

The survey was sent out at the end of January 2006, first to the 500 largest school districts in the country, then to 2,000 smaller districts. While the survey was designed to target public school districts, private and independent schools were also welcome to participate (ibid.).

> At the end of the study, we will be providing every respondent with a comprehensive set of results. They can then do a comparison of their own district with others in their state and around the country.

The researchers also plan to make the report available to state-level policymakers and commercial vendors. A major presentation on the survey results is planned for the summer of 2006 as this book was going to press. A presentation to the Chief State Officers organization is also planned. Data analysis will be crucial to making sense of all the different responses from all the different parties (ibid.):

> Once we have analyzed the data, there will be things that pop out. Half will probably reinforce what we know, half will probably be surprises. As we go through and note the surprises, we need to dig in and say, "Why are we getting this?"

For example, on questions regarding the purchase of curriculum content, researchers will need to delve into the reasons behind these purchases: Is it because of increased demand for math, science, and technology jobs? Is it because teachers are asking for more electronic media? Is this demand coming from parents and students, or are test scores behind the push?

The results of this survey will inform our planning for the future of 1-to-1 in many powerful ways.

So, Why Laptops?

We return again to the questions we started with—why laptops, and why 1-to-1? Why restructure our schools and districts, plan and develop wireless networks, purchase hardware and software, invest in professional development for teachers, hire technology leaders and technicians, and heap yet another huge initiative onto the overloaded plates of our teachers and administrators by introducing a 1-to-1 laptop program?

While every school, district, and state will need to answer this question on its own based on its overall educational mission or philosophy, the most important rationale is true for them all: the digitally enhanced, comprehensively networked world our students are entering demands it. It's a world that demands instant access to information, higher order thinking skills, and the ability to collaborate over distance. 1-to-1 provides them all—in spades. It's not easy, it's not straightforward, it's time-consuming and expensive, but it's the most important thing we can do for our kids to prepare them for the world to come.

Appendix A
SUPPORT DOCUMENTS FROM THE PECK SCHOOL'S 1-TO-1 PROGRAM

Acceptable Use Policy
for the Use of Computers and Telecommunications

THE PECK SCHOOL PROVIDES computing and network resources for students, employees, and others affiliated with The Peck School for school communication and educational use. Members of The Peck School community are encouraged to use the computers, peripheral hardware (digital cameras, scanners, DVD players, Smart Boards), software packages, electronic mail (e-mail), and software installed by Peck's technology department, for educational or school related activities and for the exchange of useful information. However, the equipment, software, and network capacities provided through The Peck School computer services are, and remain the property of, The Peck School.

Appropriate or acceptable educational uses of these resources include:

▶ The use of Peck-owned software, hardware, and the Peck Intranet for scholastic endeavor.

▶ Accessing the Internet to retrieve information from libraries, databases, and World Wide Web sites to enrich and expand curriculum.

▶ E-mail capabilities to facilitate communication and distance-learning projects.

All users are expected to conduct their online activities in an ethical and legal fashion. The use of these resources is a privilege, not a right. Misuse of these resources will result in the suspension or loss of these privileges, as well as possible disciplinary, legal, and/or monetary consequences.

Examples of inappropriate or unacceptable use(s) of these resources include, but are not limited to, those uses that violate the law, the rules of network etiquette, that are used in a manner disruptive to the work or educational environment or that hamper the integrity or security of any network connected to the Internet. Some unacceptable practices include:

▶ The use of AOL IM, iChat, Yahoo Messenger or other Instant Messaging programs while at Peck.

▶ Transmission of any material in violation of any US or state law, including but not limited to: copyrighted material; threatening, harassing, pornographic, or obscene material; or material protected by trade secret. The transmission of copyrighted materials without the written permission of the author or creator through The Peck School e-mail or other network resources in violation of US copyright law is prohibited.

▶ As with all forms of communications, e-mail or other network resources may not be used in a manner that is disruptive to the work or educational environment. The display or transmission of messages, images, cartoons or the transmission or use of e-mail or other computer messages that are sexually explicit constitute harassment which is prohibited by The Peck School. It is also illegal for anyone to knowingly allow any telecommunications facility under their control to be used for the transmission of illegal material.

▶ The use for personal financial or commercial gain, product advertisement, or the sending of unsolicited junk mail, or chain letters is prohibited.

▶ The forgery, reading, deleting, copying, or modifying of electronic mail messages of other users is prohibited.

▶ The creation, propagation, and/or use of computer viruses are prohibited.

▶ Deleting, examining, copying, or modifying files and/or data belonging to other users are prohibited.

▶ Unauthorized copying/installation of software programs belonging to the school is prohibited.

▶ Intentional destruction, deletion or disablement of Peck installed software on any computer is prohibited.

▶ Vandalism is prohibited. This includes, but is not limited to, any attempt to harm or destroy the data of another user, the network/Internet, or any networks or sites connected to the network/Internet. Attempts to breach security codes and/or passwords will also be considered a form of vandalism.

▶ Destruction of hardware or software or attempts to exceed or modify the parameters of the system is prohibited.

▶ Nothing in this policy shall prohibit The Peck School operator from intercepting and stopping e-mail messages that have the capacity to overload the computer resources.

▶ Discipline may be imposed for intentional overloading of The Peck School computer resources.

Access to The Peck School e-mail and similar electronic communication systems is a privilege and certain responsibilities accompany that privilege. The Peck School users are expected to demonstrate the same level of ethical and professional manner as is required in face-to-face or written communications. All users are required to maintain and safeguard password protected access to both personal and confidential Peck files and folders.

▶ Unauthorized attempts to access another person's e-mail or similar electronic communications or to use another's name, e-mail or computer address or workstation to send e-mail or similar electronic communications are prohibited and may subject the individual to disciplinary action. Anonymous or forged messages will be treated in violation of this policy.

▶ All users must understand that The Peck School cannot guarantee the privacy or confidentiality of electronic documents and any messages that are confidential as a matter of law should not be communicated over e-mail.

▶ The Peck School reserves the right to access e-mail to retrieve The Peck School information and records, to engage in routine computer maintenance and housekeeping, to carry out internal investigations, to check Internet access history, or to disclose messages, data or files to law enforcement authorities.

▶ Any information contained on any Peck School computer's hard drive or computer disks that were purchased by The Peck School are considered the property of The Peck School.

This agreement applies to stand-alone computers as well as computers connected to the network or Internet. Any attempt to violate the provisions of this agreement will result in revocation of the user's privileges, regardless of the success or failure of the attempt. In addition, school disciplinary action, and/or appropriate legal action may be taken. The decision of The Peck School regarding inappropriate use of the technology or telecommunication resources is final. Monetary remuneration may be sought for damage necessitating repair or replacement of equipment.

_____   _____
Peck Student Signature   Peck Parent or Guardian Signature

Acceptable Use Policy—Student Summary

Note: students need to know and follow the entire AUP. This section is an overview and a summary; all students must follow the entirety of the AUP.

Use of Peck computers, software, the network, e-mail, the Internet, and any component of information technology installed or in use at The Peck School must be:

LARK: Legal, Appropriate, Responsible, and Kind

▶ Legal: illegally copied or downloaded software, music, or games may not be used on any computer at Peck *including laptops issued to Peck students.*

▶ Appropriate: only appropriate words and images are used and viewed—if inappropriate materials are viewed or received, it is the responsibility of the recipient to see that an adult is informed.

▶ Responsible: meaning that diligent care is taken with all hardware, systems settings (including shared computer screensavers or systems files), and software, so as to prevent damage, changing, or misuse, whether intentional or not.

▶ Kind: computer use does not in any way tread on the rights or feelings of others in the Peck community.

Peck's Laptop Policy from the Parent Handbook

THE PECK SCHOOL STUDENT LAPTOP PROGRAM
LAPTOP GUIDELINES AND POLICY

Loan Period

The computers will be issued to students at the distribution/orientation session at the beginning of the school year. The computers must be returned, with all accompanying cables, drives, and other items no later than the Wednesday before commencement.

Distribution and Orientation

The distribution of laptops to students takes place at the beginning of the school year, followed by orientation sessions explaining proper care of the laptops. A parent or guardian is required to sign for the laptop and other items.

Additional instruction in the maintenance, care, transportation and proper handling of the laptops will be held in classes at the beginning of the school year.

Liability

The laptop is issued to the student who, with his or her parents or legal guardians, is the only authorized user of that computer. Although each student accepts responsibility for the care and use of the laptop, the laptop remains the sole property of the Peck School.

The Peck School owns licenses for the software installed on the laptop. Under no circumstances may any of this software be transferred to any other computer except under the direction of the Technology Department.

The Peck School purchases an extended warranty contract on all laptops. However, in the event of damage or negligence to the laptop determined by our Apple warranty provider to not be due to normal wear and tear, parents will be charged a portion of the required repair.

Case

The laptop must always be transported in a case approved by the Technology Department. It must be purchased from or issued by the Tech Department and students must keep the original luggage tag on the case. Students may personalize this bag any way they wish.

Daily Use

Students are expected to arrive at school every day with their laptop fully charged.

Network Access

Use of the Peck network is governed by the Peck School Acceptable Use Policy.

Students have a personal folder on the server accessible only to them and the Technology Department. They also have access to group folders shared by other students or teachers.

Web Access—E-mail Access

Homework assignments are located on Peck's e-mail system. FirstClass e-mail software is installed on student laptop computers.

There is also a Web version of e-mail, which should be used only when the laptop or home computer is not available, and is accessed by clicking on PeckNet.

Sports policy

A student may not take his or her laptop to away games. The student or his/her parents must make plans to transport it home.

Batteries, power adapters

Loaner batteries and power adapters will be available in the CT lab help desk. A student may borrow a battery during the day at any time by signing it out. It must be returned at the end of the day. No one may take a battery from the charger without signing it out first.

A student may sign out a power adapter to borrow from the CT lab help desk.

Any batteries or power adapters not returned will be charged to parents.

Care

Laptops should not be left in temperatures below 35 degrees or above 90 degrees.

Food, drinks, or pets should not be near the laptop to avoid damage.

Rain, wet hands, and high humidity are risky to laptops and should be avoided.

Security

The laptop should be with the student or locked in his or her locker in the CT building at all times. Unattended laptops will be "kidnapped" by faculty and taken to the Upper School Office.

Students should always guard their laptop closely. It must not be left on car seats, on benches, or anywhere that might be tempting to others.

Students who use public transportation will transport the computer inside the school-provided backpack. The computer must stay in the backpack until the student arrives home safely.

Internet and Printer Use at Home

The Technology Department will help you get your laptop to work from home to access the Internet and/or your home printer. See the Technology Department if you need this assistance and be sure to bring in any CDs or any other materials from your printer or Internet provider.

Flashcards

Parents may purchase USB flashcards which fit into the port of any newer computer, and which allow saving of files, through CDW-G. The cost for a 256Mg flashcard is $27.99, a 512Mg flashcard is $49.99. There is also a shipping cost of $5.30.

Loaner Laptops

Should the laptop become inoperable, students may come to the CT Computer Lab and borrow a loaner while his or her laptop is being repaired.

Backing Up

Students are responsible for backing up their personal files to Peck's computer network. Server files are backed up and saved on tape every night.

Troubleshooting

Students should report any laptop problems right away to the teacher in the class or to the Technology Department.

Damage

All physical damage to the laptop must be reported immediately to a responsible adult—either at home or at school. It then must be reported to the Technology Department as soon as possible. The Technology Department will arrange for repair and a loaner as needed.

Damages not covered by our Apple warranty will be partly charged to parents.

Software/Printing Problems

Students should see the Technology Department with any software, printing, or other problems.

TO ACCESS PECK SCHOOL E-MAIL FOR 5–8 HOMEWORK ASSIGNMENTS AND THE TESTS AND MAJOR WORKS CALENDARS

All homework for Grade 5 through Grade 8 students is accessible from student e-mail. Students do the following:

1. Doubleclick to access e-mail. Type your ID and password.

2. Doubleclick on the folder for the subject, e.g., math.

3. Doubleclick to see homework assignments.

There is also a calendar for tests and major work, which students may view from their e-mail desktops by doubleclicking on the calendar.

Parents may access the same class assignments and tests and major work calendars from The Peck School Web site.

Seventh-Grade Laptop Program—FAQ (Frequently Asked Questions)

Note: This FAQ form is for new seventh-graders getting laptops for the first time

Congratulations. Being given a laptop computer means we think you are ready for this responsibility. We expect using a laptop will be very helpful for studying, organizing, and learning.

Q: When do I receive my Peck Laptop?

A: You will receive your Peck-issued laptop computer on the second day of school, Friday, September 9, for use in school. We'll also have sessions about using and caring for your laptop.

Q: What do my parents have to do in order for me to get my laptop?

A: Your parents need to provide you with a check for $165 for the first day of school. They (and you) also have to sign the green assessment sheet and the Peck Acceptable Use Policy for you to return the next day.

Q: What if I can't purchase the case the first day?

A: You need to purchase the case to get your laptop so you won't have a laptop right away. Once you can purchase the case, you will get your laptop. It's really important the laptop be transported in the proper case.

Q: May I use my own case?

A: No, you have to use the case your parents will purchase for you. We have investigated cases and have found that the one you are purchasing is the best and minimizes possible damage.

Q: May I use the case from my brother/sister/friend who graduated from Peck and had a Peck-issued case?

A: Yes, you may use that case if you have it. You must bring it to Peck the first day of school.

Q: May I decorate my case?

A: Yes, it's yours, go ahead and decorate it. Of course, be sure there is nothing inappropriate or offensive about how you decorate the case.

Q: Who owns the laptop?

A: Peck School owns the laptop computer, not you and not your parents. It is therefore very important that you take good care of it, leave the tags in place, don't damage it or write on it, as it doesn't actually belong to you.

Q: May I take the laptop home?

A: Yes, once the two forms (green assessment sheet and Peck Acceptable Use Policy) are signed, you will be able to take your laptop home. It's important that you have these forms signed first, however, so until the forms are signed, your laptop will stay at Peck.

Q: May I access the Internet and my printer at home with my laptop?

A: If you want to use the computer for the Internet and your printer at home, try first to install the correct software and see if you can make it work. If you have any problems with this, come to Mrs. Livingston and Mrs. Maguire's office for help. Be sure to bring any CD's, manuals, and the name and model of your printer, or the name of your Internet provider.

Q: What do I do if my laptop doesn't work or is damaged?

A: See the Tech Department as soon as possible. It's important not to delay as one problem can lead to another if not solved right away. If your computer is damaged, we will try to fix it or send it out for repair. If it needs to be repaired, we will loan you a computer to use until it's returned.

Q: May I put games or software on the laptop?

A: Any games, software, or music that you have legally purchased may be put on your laptop. However, if anything you install causes the computer to not function, your computer may have to be reformatted. This means all files will be lost. So take care that you don't install too many files or software programs as you could fill up the hard drive or cause problems.

Q: How do I carry my laptop?

A: Always carry your laptop in its case, even when at home. The hinge on the laptop can become damaged if you carry it open and the risk of tripping or dropping the computer exists if you don't have it in the case.

Q: Where do I keep my laptop at school?

A: At school, you will use your laptop for nearly all your classes. For any classes not requiring your laptop, or during lunch, you must store your laptop in your cubby and thread the cable/lock we will give you through the handle of your laptop case and through the loop affixed to your cubby, and lock the lock. If you do not do this, you run the risk of having your laptop *"kidnapped"* by Peck faculty or administrators. We do this to make the point that you must be responsible for the laptop and never leave it unattended or unlocked.

Q: Is there anything special I should do with my laptop at home?

A: Just be sure you plug it in overnight so you come to Peck with a fully charged battery. Also, you should always print your papers from home to eliminate the early morning "bottleneck" at Peck printers.

Q: What else should I know or read?

A: You and your parents should thoroughly read the Technology Appendix that will be given to you the first day of school. There is an entire section about the laptop program. This appendix also contains the Peck Acceptable Use Policy, which you and your parents must sign, and understand.

Q: How long do I have my laptop?

A: The laptop is yours to use during seventh and eighth grade at Peck. Over the summer, we collect the computers, and reformat them. Once school starts up again, you will get your laptop back.

Q: What if I have any other questions or problems with my laptop?

A: Come by the office where Mrs. Maguire and Mrs. Livingston are in the lower floor of CT. We are there every recess and somewhere around the school (fixing computers) every day. You can also send an e-mail to Tech Support, or to Mrs. Livingston.

THE PECK SCHOOL LAPTOP PROGRAM—ASSESSMENT

SCHOOL YEAR: 2005–2006

Inventory Info		Student Info	
iBook #	701	Student Last Name	sample
serial #	UV32204DNDF	Student First Name	sample
		Lock #	26
security #	USF81113	Lock Combination	xxx-xxx
		Cubby #	28

Items and Condition (Please Circle)

Top Case:	Excellent	OK	Poor/Explain: _____
Bottom Case:	Excellent	OK	Poor/Explain: _____
Screen:	Excellent	OK	Poor/Explain: _____
Keyboard:	Excellent	OK	Poor/Explain: _____
Power Port:	Excellent	OK	Poor/Explain: _____
Trackpad:	Excellent	OK	Poor/Explain: _____
Other:	Excellent	OK	Poor/Explain: _____

I hereby accept responsibility for the care of this laptop computer. If it is damaged or lost while in my care, I understand that I may be charged for its repair or replacement.

Student Signature: _____ Date: _____

Parent Signature: _____ Date: _____

Tech Dept. Signature: _____ Date: _____

JUMP TO INVENTORY

Appendix B
REFERENCES AND RESOURCES

Literature

Apple Learning Interchange. (n.d.). *The Maine idea: A computer for every lap*. Retrieved January 15, 2005, from http://ali.apple.com/ali_sites/glefli/exhibits/1001165/A_Computer_for_Every_Lap.html

Barrios, Tina. (2004, March 22). *Laptops for learning: Final report and recommendations of the Laptops for Learning Task Force*. Retrieved December 21, 2005, from University of South Florida, Educational Technology Clearing House Web site: http://etc.usf.edu/L4L/Cover.pdf

Britto, J., Fish, T., & Throckmorton, A. (2002). *Leadership and technology at independent schools: A handbook for school leaders in administration, technology, and academics*. Washington, DC: National Association of Independent Schools.

Brown, John Seely. (2001). *Learning in the digital age*. Paper presented at the Forum for the Future of Higher Education, Aspen, CO. Retrieved January 21, 2006, from www.educause.edu/ir/library/pdf/ffpiu015.pdf

Cuban, L. (2001). *Oversold and underused: Computers in the classroom*. Cambridge, MA: Harvard University Press.

Dickard, Norris (Ed.). (2003). *The sustainability challenge: Taking edtech to the next level* (Benton Foundation and the Education Development Center's Center for Children and Technology, Internet document). Retrieved January 4, 2005, from www.Benton.org/publibrary/sustainability/sus_challenge.html

Dewey, J. (1902). *The school and society and the child and the curriculum*. Chicago and London: University of Chicago Press.

Edwards, Mark A. (2004, February 1). Fulfilling the promise of ed tech: Laptops spur learning. *eSchool news*. Retrieved January 2, 2006, from www.eschoolnews.com/news/showstory.cfm?ArticleID=4848

Fairman, J. (2004, May). *Trading roles: Teachers and students learn with technology* (Maine Learning Technology Initiative Research Report #3). Retrieved November 27, 2004, from www.state.me.us/mlte/

Fullan, Michael. (2001). *Leading in a culture of change*. San Francisco: Jossey-Bass.

Garthwait, A., & Weller, H. (2004, July). *Two teachers implement one-to-one computing: A case study* (Maine Learning Technology Initiative Research Report #5). Retrieved November 30, 2004, from www.state.me.us/mlte/

Gladwell, Malcolm. (2000). *The tipping point: How little things can make a big difference.* Boston: Bay Back Books.

Goldberg, A., Russell, M., & Cook, A. (2002). *Meta-analysis: Writing with computers 1992–2002.* Retrieved June 23, 2006, from inTASC Web site: www.bc.edu/research/intasc/publications.shtml

Gulek, J. C., & Demirtas, H. (2005). Learning with technology: The impact of laptop use on student achievement. *Journal of Technology, Learning, and Assessment, 3*(2). Available from http://www.jtla.org

Hill, J., & Reeves, T. (2004). *Change takes time: The promise of ubiquitous computing in schools* (Athens Academy, Athens, Georgia, 4-year evaluation report). Retrieved December 10, 2004, from http://lpsl.coe.uga.edu/projects/aalaptop/pdf/finalreport.pdf

Jonassen, D., Peck, K., & Wilson, B. (1999). *Learning with technology: A constructivist perspective.* Upper Saddle River, NJ: Merrill Prentice Hall.

Kim, Ann S. (2002, September 6). The whole world is watching you. *Maine Today.* Retrieved January 2, 2006, from http://news.mainetoday.com/indepth/laptops/020906laptops.shtml

Knowles, M. S. (1975). *Self-directed learning: A guide for learners and teachers.* Englewood Cliffs, NJ: Prentice Hall/Cambridge.

Knowles, M. S. (1984). *Andragogy in action: Applying modern principles of adult education.* San Francisco: Jossey-Bass.

Kousez, J., Posner, B. (1995). *The leadership challenge: How to keep getting extraordinary things done in organizations.* San Francisco: Jossey-Bass.

Lane, Dawn M. (2003, April). *Early evidence from the field: Impact on students and learning* (Maine Learning Technology Initiative Occasional Paper #1). Retrieved November 15, 2004, from www.state.me.us/mlte/

Lenhart, A., Simon, M., & Graziano, M. (2001, September). *The Internet and education.* Retrieved December 23, 2004, from the Pew Internet & American Life Project Web site: http://www.pewinternet.org/pdfs/PIP_Schools_Report.pdf

Levin, D., & Arafe, S. (2002, August 14). *The digital disconnect: The widening gap between Internet-savvy students and their schools.* Retrieved December 19, 2004, from the Pew Internet & American Life Project Web site: www.pewInternet.org

Levin, Howard. (2005, December/January). Reflections on the effects of one-to-one computing in a high school. *Learning and Leading with Technology, 33*(4), 17–20.

Levine, Mel. (2002). *A mind at a time.* New York: Simon & Shuster.

Light, D., McDermott, M., & Honey, M. (2002, May). *Project Hiller: The impact of ubiquitous portable technology on an urban school.* Retrieved June 23, 2006, from the Center for Children and Technology Web site: www2.edc.org/CCT/publications_report_summary.asp?numPubId=129

Livingston, P. (2004). *7th Graders and 24/7.* Unpublished master's thesis, Chestnut Hill College, Philadelphia.

Morrison, Elizabeth Donnell. (1992). *Because they cared.* Morristown, NJ: The Peck School.

Muir, M., Manchester, B., & Moulton, J. (2004, July). Maine learns: The four keys to success of the first statewide learning with laptops initiative. *T H E Journal.* Available online at http://thejournal.com

Muir, M., Manchester, B., & Moulton, J. (2005, Summer). Special topic: Learning with laptops. *Educational Leadership, 62.* Available online at www.ascd.org

Nair, Prakash. (2000). *The student laptop computer in classrooms: Not just a tool.* Retrieved January 2, 2005, from www.designshare.com/Research/Nair/Laptop_Classrooms.htm

Papert, S. (2003, July/August). Creativity can be hard fun *Frames.* Retrieved June 23, 2006, from http://frames.media.mit.edu/frames.nsf/f0f612c016af385185256d200053e19942a05ebfb77df16085256d90005badf5?OpenDocument#

Parsad, B., & Jones, J. (2005). *Internet access in U.S. public schools and classrooms: 1994-2003* (NCES 2005015). Washington, DC: National Center for Educational Statistics.

Peterson, Shane. (2000, January 15). *King of Maine.* Retrieved December 23, 2005, from www.govtech.net/magazine/story.php?id=3194&issue=1:2000

Restak, R. (2001). *Mozart's brain and the fighter pilot: Unleashing your brain's potential.* New York: Harmony.

Rockman, S. (2003, Fall). Learning from laptops. *Threshold.* Retrieved November 29, 2004, from Cable in the Classroom Web site: www.ciconline.org

Rockman *et al.* (2000). *A more complex picture: Laptop use and impact in the context of changing home and school access.* Retrieved March 15, 2005, from http://rockman.com/projects/projectDetail.php?id=126

Rockman *et al.* (2004, April 14). *Year three: Students at center of learning.* Retrieved December 30, 2004, from www.microsoft.com/education/AALResearch3.aspx

Sargent, K. (2003, April). *What is the impact on teacher beliefs and instructional practices?* (Maine Learning Technology Initiative Occasional Paper #3). Retrieved November 14, 2004, from www.state.me.us/mlte/

Silvernail, D. L., & Harris, W. J. (2003, March). *Teacher, student, and school perspectives* (Maine Learning Technology Initiative Mid-Year Evaluation Report). Retrieved December 15, 2004, from http://mainegov-images.informe.org/mlte/articles/research/Mid-Year%20Evaluation2003.pdf

Silvernail, D. L., & Lane, D. M. M. (2004, February). *The impact of Maine's one-to-one laptop program on middle school teachers and students. Phase one summary evidence* (Maine Education Policy Research Institute Research Report #1). Retrieved November 15, 2004, from www.state.me.us/mlte/

Solomon, G. (Ed.). (2005). 1:1 computing: A guidebook to help you make the right decisions [Special section]. *Technology & Learning.* Retrieved from http://download. microsoft.com/download/8/d/c/8dc3ebfe-6849-4534-a4b7-846a8c327874/HP1to1Guide. pdf

Stevenson, K. R. (1999, November). *Evaluation Report—Year 3, Middle School Laptop Program* (Executive Summary, Beaufort County School District, Beaufort, South Carolina). Retrieved December 15, 2004, from www.beaufort.k12.sc.us/district/ evalreport3.htm

U.S. Department of Education. (2004). *Toward a new golden age in American education: How the Internet, the law and today's students are revolutionizing expectations* (National Educational Technology Plan). Washington, DC: Author, Office of Educational Technology. Available at www.ed.gov/about/offices/list/os/technology/plan/2004/ plan.pdf

Weiser, Mark.(1993). *Some computer science issues in ubiquitous computing.* Retrieved December 22, 2004, from www.ubiq.com/hypertext/weiser/UbiCACM.html

WestEd. (2002, August). *Investing in technology: The learning return.* Retrieved November 9, 2004, from www.wested.org

Zucker, A. A., & McGhee, R. (2005, February). *A study of one-to-one computer use in mathematics and science instruction at the secondary level in Henrico County public schools.* Retrieved March 10, 2005, from http://ubiqcomputing.org/FinalReport.pdf

Web

Case Study Teaching in Science: http://ublib.buffalo.edu/libraries/projects/cases/case.html

The Case-Based Teaching Architecture: www.engines4ed.org/hyperbook/nodes/ NODE-196-pg.html

Concepts to Classroom: www.thirteen.org/edonline/concept2class/inquiry/

The Institute of the Learning Sciences: creANIMate: www.engines4ed.org/hyperbook/ movies/crean.mov (imovie)

Oliver, K. (2002). Teaching Models: www.edtech.vt.edu/edtech/id/models/

Using Cases in Teaching: http://tlt.its.psu.edu/suggestions/cases/

Professional Development Conferences

Building Learning Communities. Alan November. July, Boston.
www.novemberlearning.com/Default.aspx?tabid=29

Christa McAuliffe Technology Conference. www.nhcmtc.org

Connecticut Association of Independent Schools (CAIS). Holds a summer technology conference at a Connecticut boarding school. Excellent sessions and opportunities for sharing and networking. www.cais.org

Consortium for School Networking (CosN). www.cosn.org

EdACCESS. Technical conference for small independent K–12 schools and small colleges. Moves every 2 years to a different boarding school. Not about laptops in schools but provides lots of great technical information for participants. Small and grass roots in nature. www.edaccess.org

Florida Educational Technology Conference (FETC). www.fetc.org

Lausanne Collegiate Laptop Institute. Laptops in schools conference for public, private, and parochial schools. Has keynote speakers, panels, and concurrent sessions. Has grown every year. Highly recommended. http://laptopinstitute.com

National Association of Independent Schools (NAIS). Yearly conference. Independent school organization geared toward school heads, but if you are a head and already attending, there are also technology vendors and some sessions that deal with school technology issues. www.nais.org

National Educational Computing Conference (NECC). Sponsored by ISTE (International Society for Technology in Education) and moves to different locales every year. Very extensive conference that has lately held a laptop track. Highly recommended. www.neccsite.org

National School Board's Technology + Learning + Leadership Conference. www.nsba.org/t+l/

New Jersey Educational Computing Consortium (NJECC). Regular workshops and meetings and a yearly conference for New Jersey public, private, and parochial schools. www.njecc.org

New York Association of Independent Schools (NYSAIS). Yearly technology in schools conference. November, at Mohonk in New York. Well-attended and positively recommended. www.nysais.org

One-to-One, One for All Symposium. By invitation only. For existing one-to-one schools and districts. www.irvingisd.net/symposium2005/about.htm

TCEA—TX. Computer Education Association. February, Austin, Texas. www.tcea.org

TIES Conference. http://tchlrn.ties.k12.mn.us/ties2005/main/details.asp

WEMA (Wisconsin Educational Media Association) and Brainstorm Conference. www.wemaonline.org/ev.cf.2006.about.cfm

Appendix C
NATIONAL EDUCATIONAL TECHNOLOGY STANDARDS

National Educational Technology Standards for Students (NETS•S)

The National Educational Technology Standards for students are divided into six broad categories. Standards within each category are to be introduced, reinforced, and mastered by students. Teachers can use these standards as guidelines for planning technology-based activities in which students achieve success in learning, communication, and life skills.

1. **Basic operations and concepts**

   ▶ Students demonstrate a sound understanding of the nature and operation of technology systems.

   ▶ Students are proficient in the use of technology.

2. **Social, ethical, and human issues**

   ▶ Students understand the ethical, cultural, and societal issues related to technology.

   ▶ Students practice responsible use of technology systems, information, and software.

   ▶ Students develop positive attitudes toward technology uses that support lifelong learning, collaboration, personal pursuits, and productivity.

3. **Technology productivity tools**

   ▶ Students use technology tools to enhance learning, increase productivity, and promote creativity.

   ▶ Students use productivity tools to collaborate in constructing technology-enhanced models, preparing publications, and producing other creative works.

4. **Technology communications tools**

   ▶ Students use telecommunications to collaborate, publish, and interact with peers, experts, and other audiences.

   ▶ Students use a variety of media and formats to communicate information and ideas effectively to multiple audiences.

5. **Technology research tools**

   ▶ Students use technology to locate, evaluate, and collect information from a variety of sources.

   ▶ Students use technology tools to process data and report results.

   ▶ Students evaluate and select new information resources and technological innovations based on the appropriateness to specific tasks.

6. **Technology problem-solving and decision-making tools**

   ▶ Students use technology resources for solving problems and making informed decisions.

   ▶ Students employ technology in the development of strategies for solving problems in the real world.

National Educational Technology Standards for Teachers (NETS•T)

All classroom teachers should be prepared to meet the following standards and performance indicators.

I. Technology Operations and Concepts

Teachers demonstrate a sound understanding of technology operations and concepts. Teachers:

A. demonstrate introductory knowledge, skills, and understanding of concepts related to technology (as described in the ISTE National Educational Technology Standards for Students).

B. demonstrate continual growth in technology knowledge and skills to stay abreast of current and emerging technologies.

II. Planning and Designing Learning Environments and Experiences

Teachers plan and design effective learning environments and experiences supported by technology. Teachers:

A. design developmentally appropriate learning opportunities that apply technology-enhanced instructional strategies to support the diverse needs of learners.

B. apply current research on teaching and learning with technology when planning learning environments and experiences.

C. identify and locate technology resources and evaluate them for accuracy and suitability.

D. plan for the management of technology resources within the context of learning activities.

E. plan strategies to manage student learning in a technology-enhanced environment.

III. Teaching, Learning, and the Curriculum

Teachers implement curriculum plans that include methods and strategies for applying technology to maximize student learning. Teachers:

A. facilitate technology-enhanced experiences that address content standards and student technology standards.

B. use technology to support learner-centered strategies that address the diverse needs of students.

C. apply technology to develop students' higher order skills and creativity.

D. manage student learning activities in a technology-enhanced environment.

IV. Assessment and Evaluation

Teachers apply technology to facilitate a variety of effective assessment and evaluation strategies. Teachers:

A. apply technology in assessing student learning of subject matter using a variety of assessment techniques.

B. use technology resources to collect and analyze data, interpret results, and communicate findings to improve instructional practice and maximize student learning.

C. apply multiple methods of evaluation to determine students' appropriate use of technology resources for learning, communication, and productivity.

V. Productivity and Professional Practice

Teachers use technology to enhance their productivity and professional practice. Teachers:

A. use technology resources to engage in ongoing professional development and lifelong learning.

B. continually evaluate and reflect on professional practice to make informed decisions regarding the use of technology in support of student learning.

C. apply technology to increase productivity.

D. use technology to communicate and collaborate with peers, parents, and the larger community in order to nurture student learning.

VI. Social, Ethical, Legal, and Human Issues

Teachers understand the social, ethical, legal, and human issues surrounding the use of technology in PK–12 schools and apply that understanding in practice. Teachers:

A. model and teach legal and ethical practice related to technology use.

B. apply technology resources to enable and empower learners with diverse backgrounds, characteristics, and abilities.

C. identify and use technology resources that affirm diversity.

D. promote safe and healthy use of technology resources.

E. facilitate equitable access to technology resources for all students.

National Educational Technology Standards for Administrators (NETS•A)

All school administrators should be prepared to meet the following standards and performance indicators. These standards are a national consensus among educational stakeholders regarding what best indicates effective school leadership for comprehensive and appropriate use of technology in schools.

I.   **Leadership and Vision—Educational leaders inspire a shared vision for comprehensive integration of technology and foster an environment and culture conducive to the realization of that vision. Educational leaders:**

   A. facilitate the shared development by all stakeholders of a vision for technology use and widely communicate that vision.

   B. maintain an inclusive and cohesive process to develop, implement, and monitor a dynamic, long-range, and systemic technology plan to achieve the vision.

   C. foster and nurture a culture of responsible risk taking and advocate policies promoting continuous innovation with technology.

   D. use data in making leadership decisions.

   E. advocate for research-based effective practices in use of technology.

   F. advocate, on the state and national levels, for policies, programs, and funding opportunities that support implementation of the district technology plan.

II. **Learning and Teaching—Educational leaders ensure that curricular design, instructional strategies, and learning environments integrate appropriate technologies to maximize learning and teaching. Educational leaders:**

   A. identify, use, evaluate, and promote appropriate technologies to enhance and support instruction and standards-based curriculum leading to high levels of student achievement.

   B. facilitate and support collaborative technology-enriched learning environments conducive to innovation for improved learning.

   C. provide for learner-centered environments that use technology to meet the individual and diverse needs of learners.

   D. facilitate the use of technologies to support and enhance instructional methods that develop higher-level thinking, decision-making, and problem-solving skills.

   E. provide for and ensure that faculty and staff take advantage of quality professional learning opportunities for improved learning and teaching with technology.

III. **Productivity and Professional Practice—Educational leaders apply technology to enhance their professional practice and to increase their own productivity and that of others. Educational leaders:**

   A. model the routine, intentional, and effective use of technology.

   B. employ technology for communication and collaboration among colleagues, staff, parents, students, and the larger community.

   C. create and participate in learning communities that stimulate, nurture, and support faculty and staff in using technology for improved productivity.

D. engage in sustained, job-related professional learning using technology resources.

E. maintain awareness of emerging technologies and their potential uses in education.

F. use technology to advance organizational improvement.

IV. Support, Management, and Operations—Educational leaders ensure the integration of technology to support productive systems for learning and administration. Educational leaders:

A. develop, implement, and monitor policies and guidelines to ensure compatibility of technologies.

B. implement and use integrated technology-based management and operations systems.

C. allocate financial and human resources to ensure complete and sustained implementation of the technology plan.

D. integrate strategic plans, technology plans, and other improvement plans and policies to align efforts and leverage resources.

E. implement procedures to drive continuous improvements of technology systems and to support technology-replacement cycles.

V. Assessment and Evaluation—Educational leaders use technology to plan and implement comprehensive systems of effective assessment and evaluation. Educational leaders:

A. use multiple methods to assess and evaluate appropriate uses of technology resources for learning, communication, and productivity.

B. use technology to collect and analyze data, interpret results, and communicate findings to improve instructional practice and student learning.

C. assess staff knowledge, skills, and performance in using technology and use results to facilitate quality professional development and to inform personnel decisions.

D. use technology to assess, evaluate, and manage administrative and operational systems.

VI. Social, Legal, and Ethical Issues—Educational leaders understand the social, legal, and ethical issues related to technology and model responsible decision making related to these issues. Educational leaders:

A. ensure equity of access to technology resources that enable and empower all learners and educators.

B. identify, communicate, model, and enforce social, legal, and ethical practices to promote responsible use of technology.

C. promote and enforce privacy, security, and online safety related to the use of technology.

D. promote and enforce environmentally safe and healthy practices in the use of technology.

E. participate in the development of policies that clearly enforce copyright law and assign ownership of intellectual property developed with district resources.

This material was originally produced as a project of the Technology Standards for School Administrators Collaborative.